Magical Moments:

Color for Joy

Inspiring Mandalas Coloring Book

Susan Apurado

ISBN 978-1540898487

First printed by Createspace 2016
USA

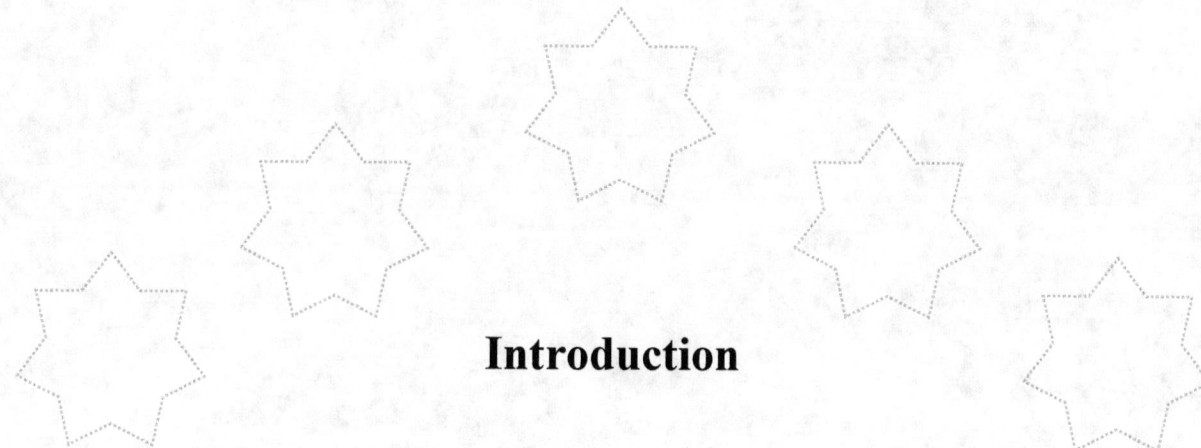

Introduction

In the hustle and bustle of day-to-day life, may you find a healthy way to slow down.

Have a spare time to sit back and relax, smell the flowers, and replenish your soul. These

hand-inked illustrations, Magical Moments: Color for Joy, which have been heartily designed to

create a magical moment, and discover your inner peace, and beauty within.

I hope you will enjoy coloring, and bringing your mind to a state of relaxation,

peace, and joy.

Life is a breeze full of vibrant colors.

Susan Apurado

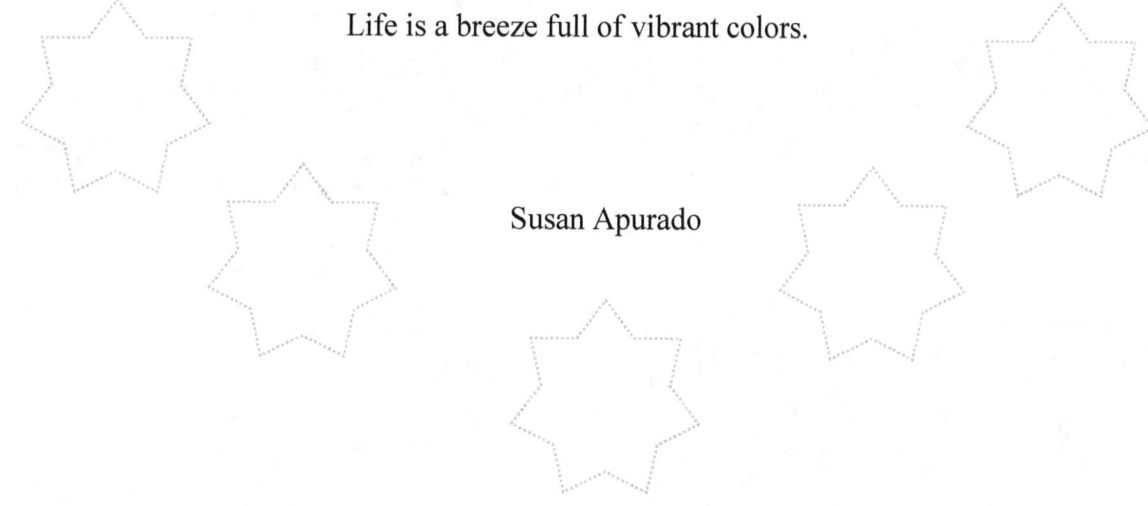

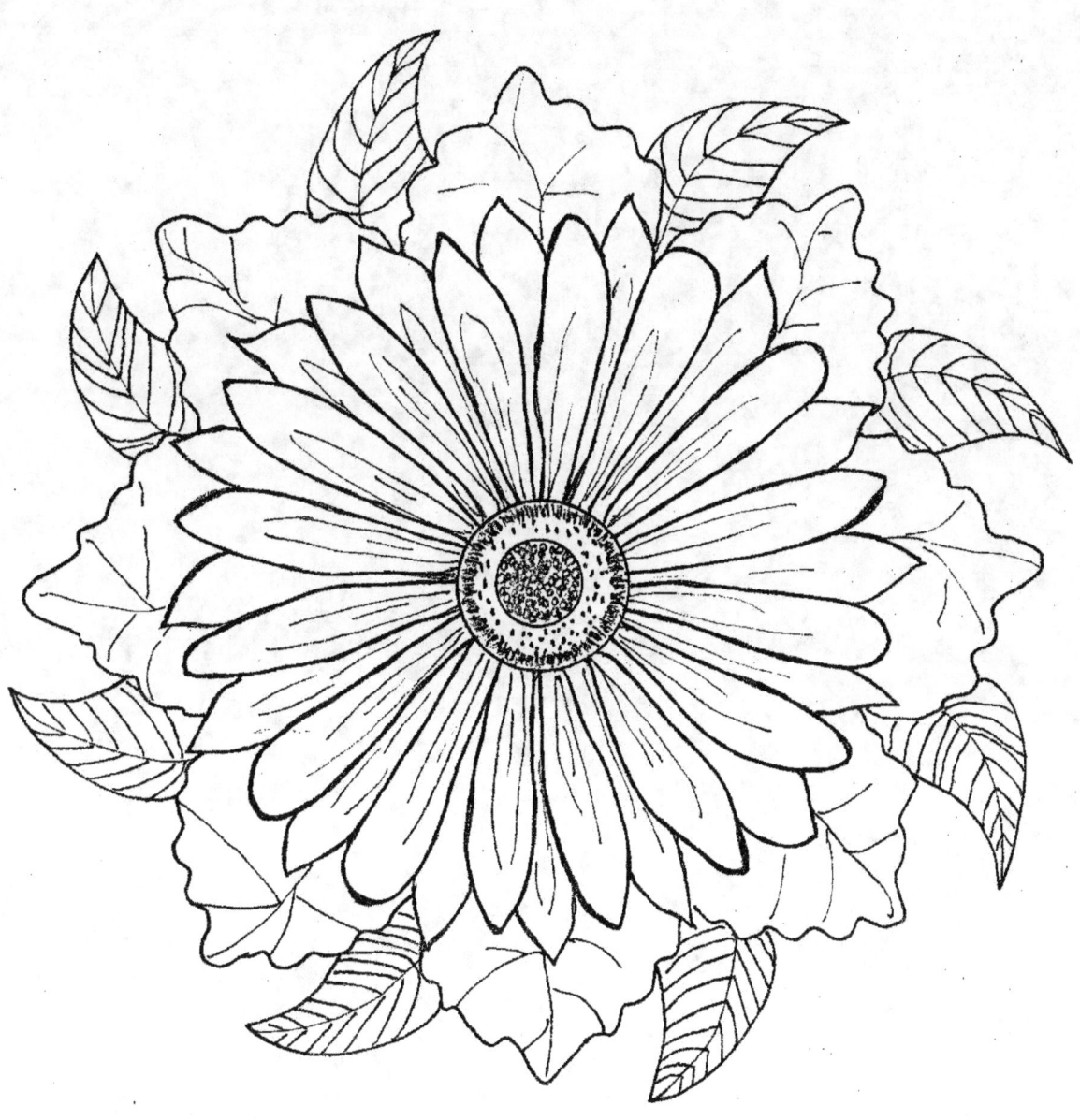

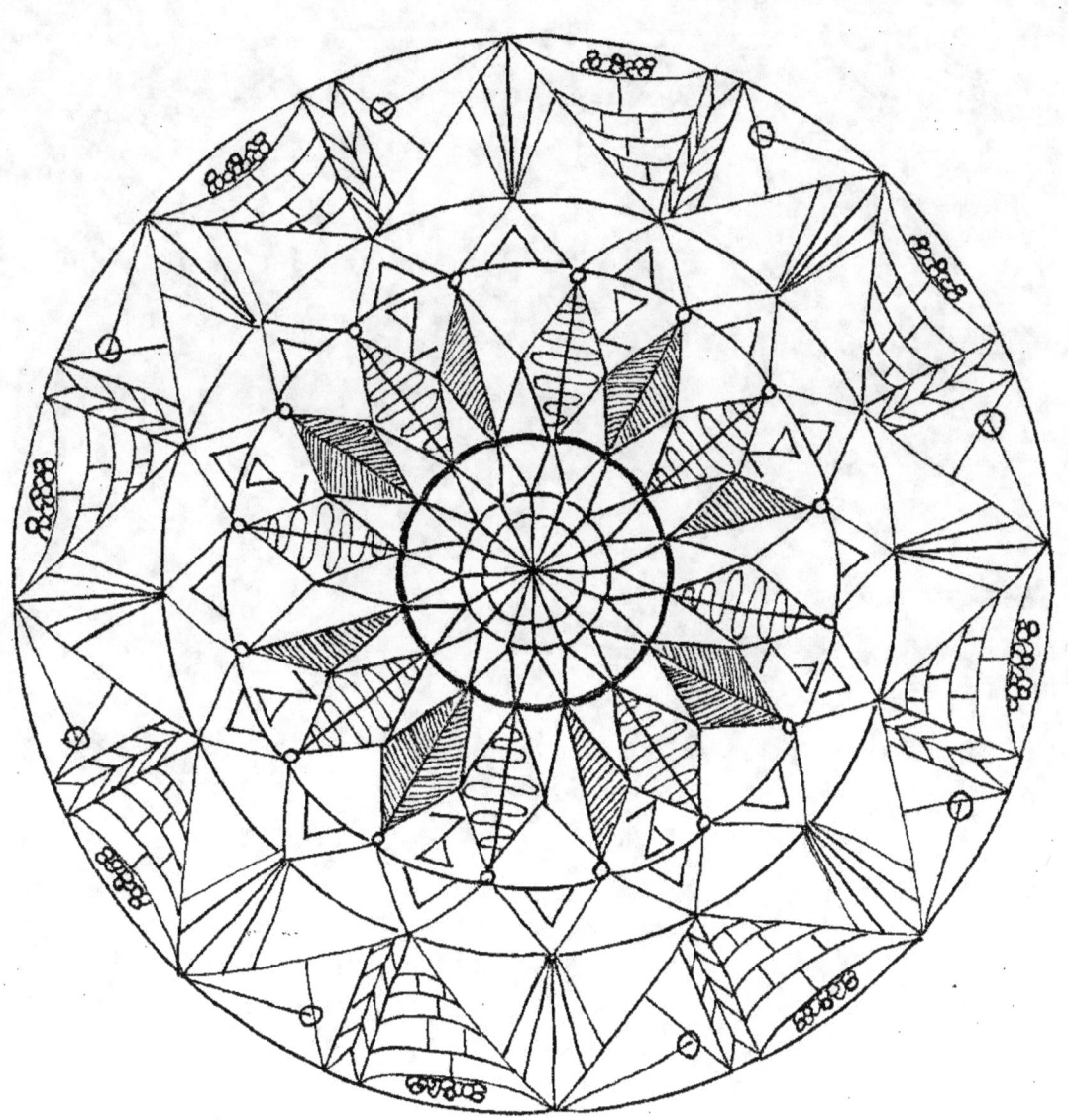

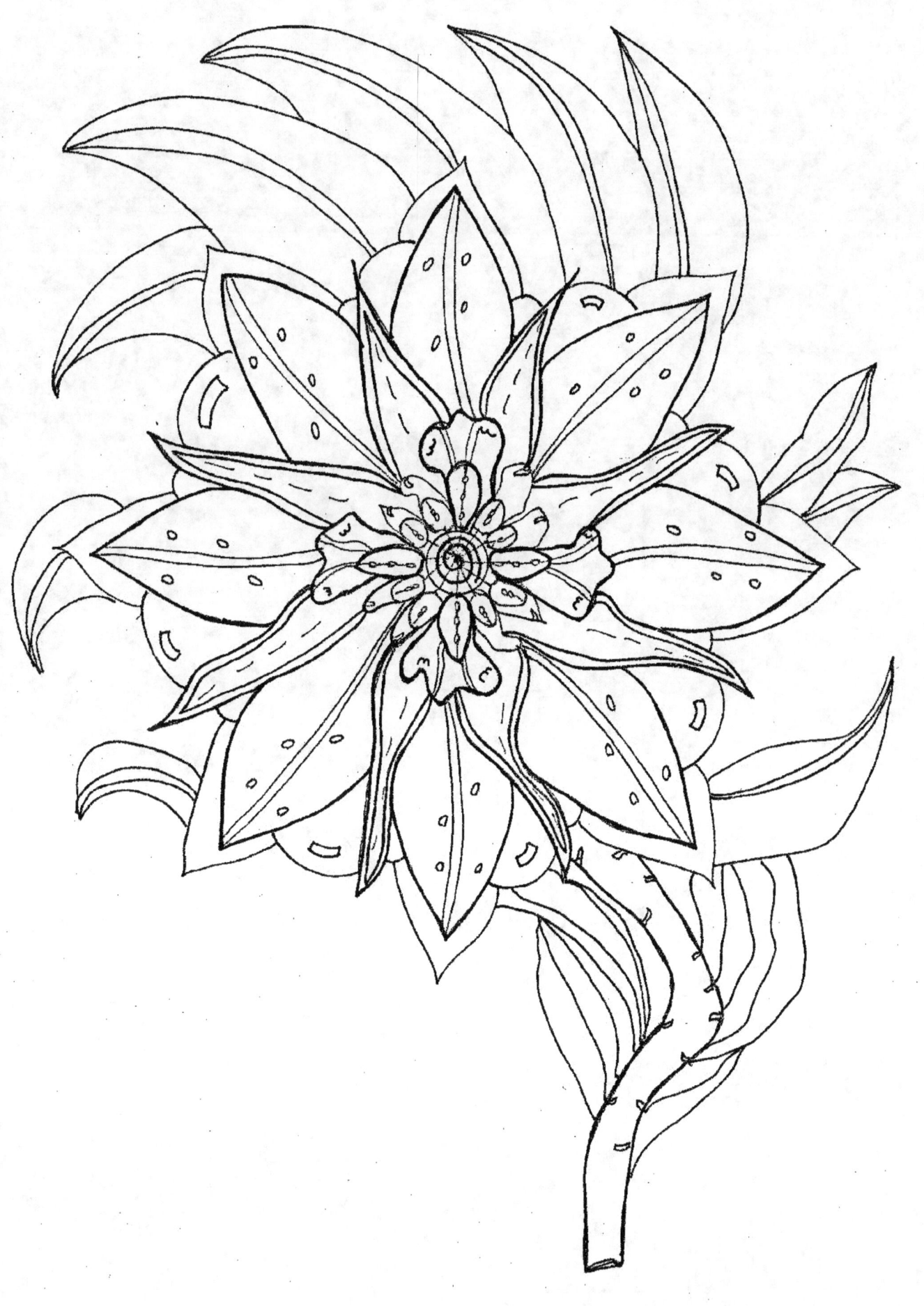

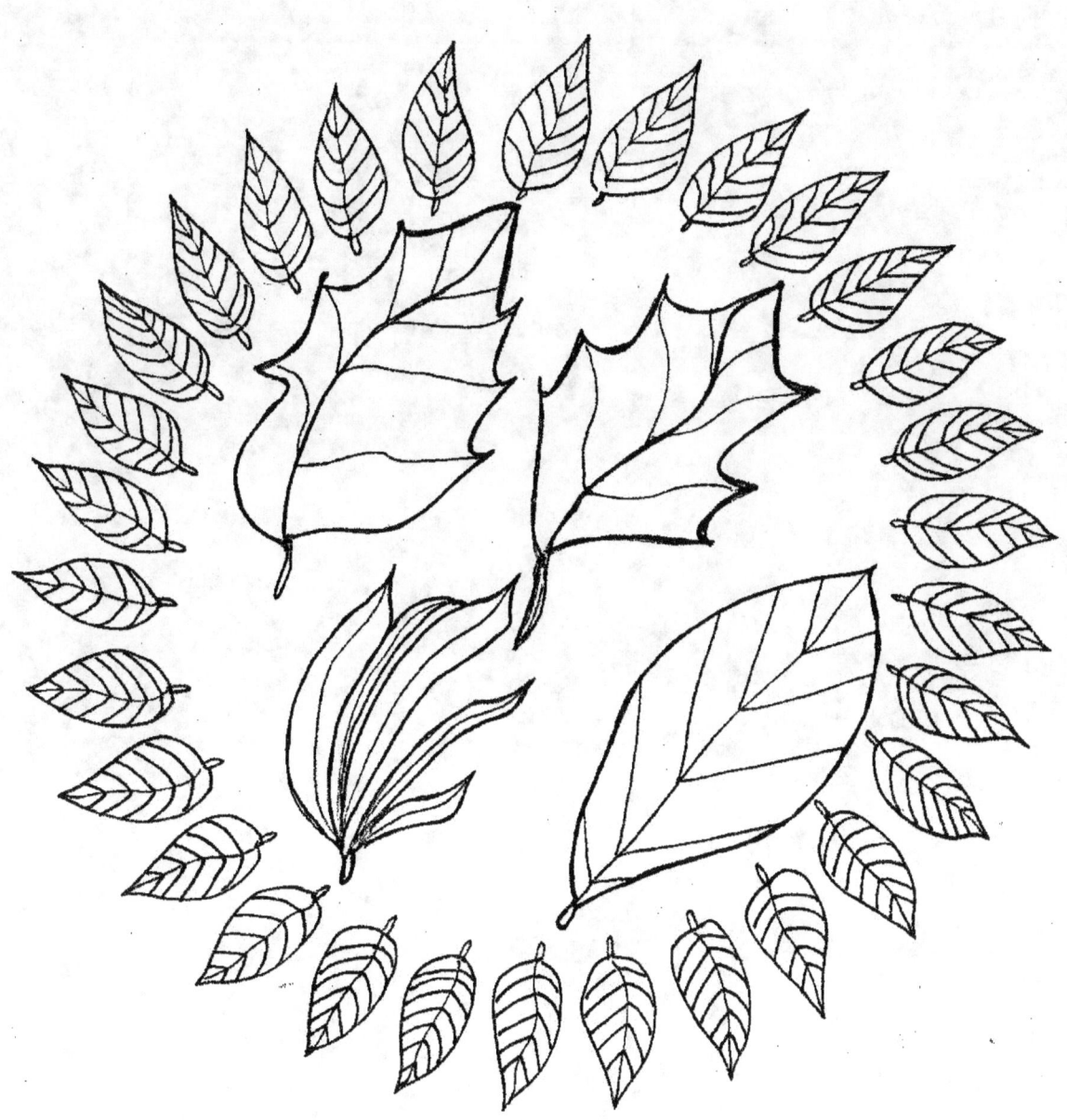

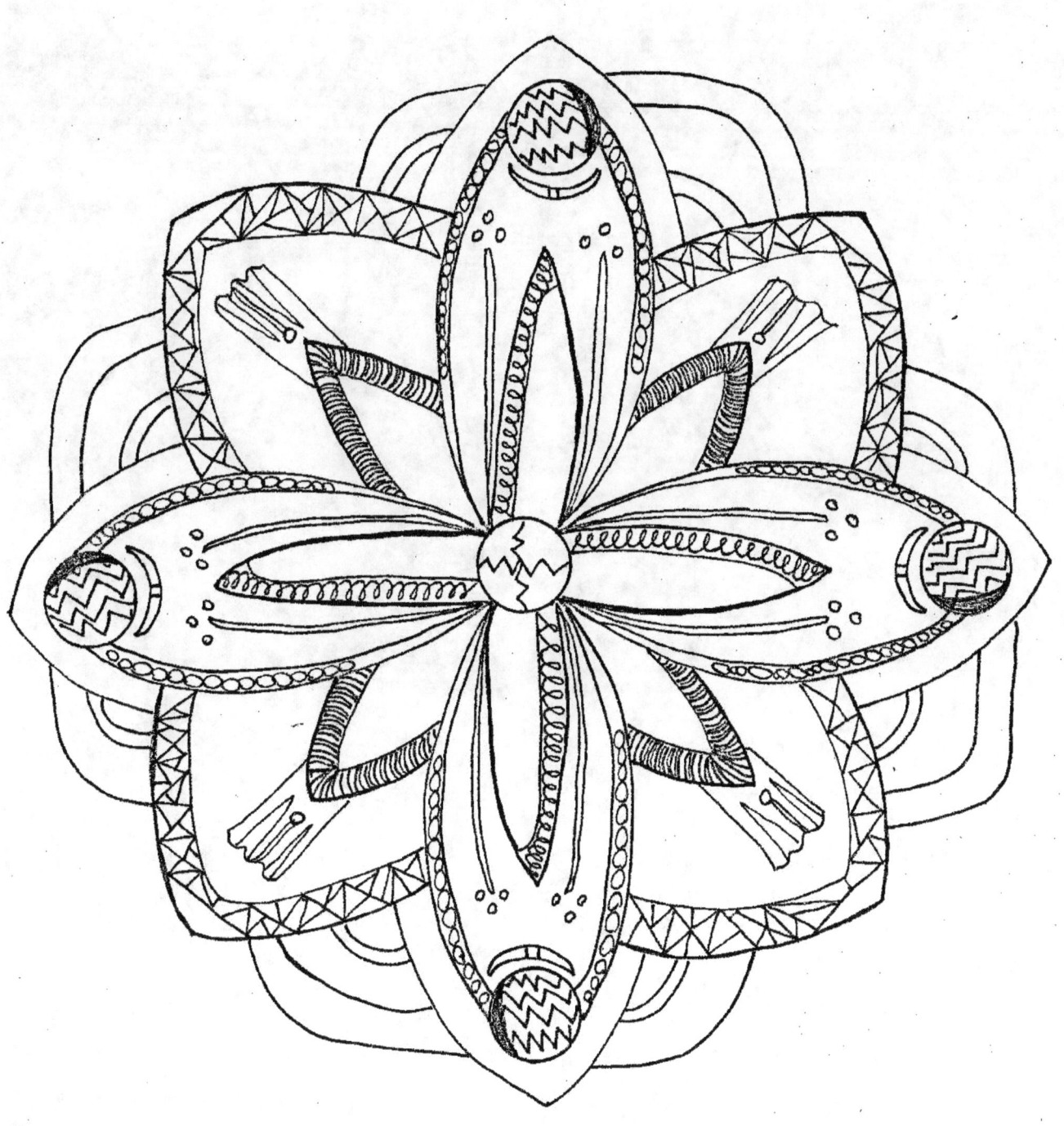

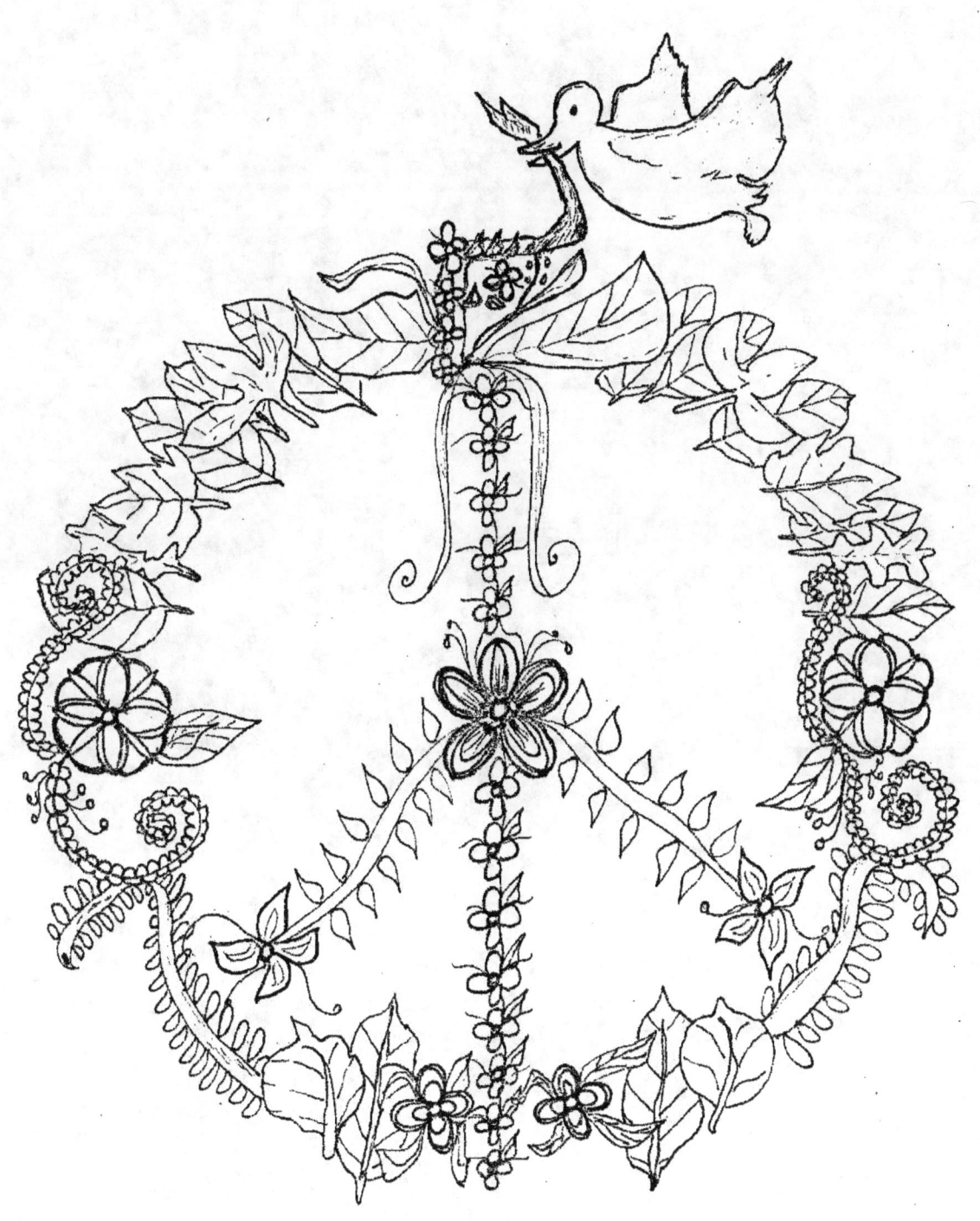

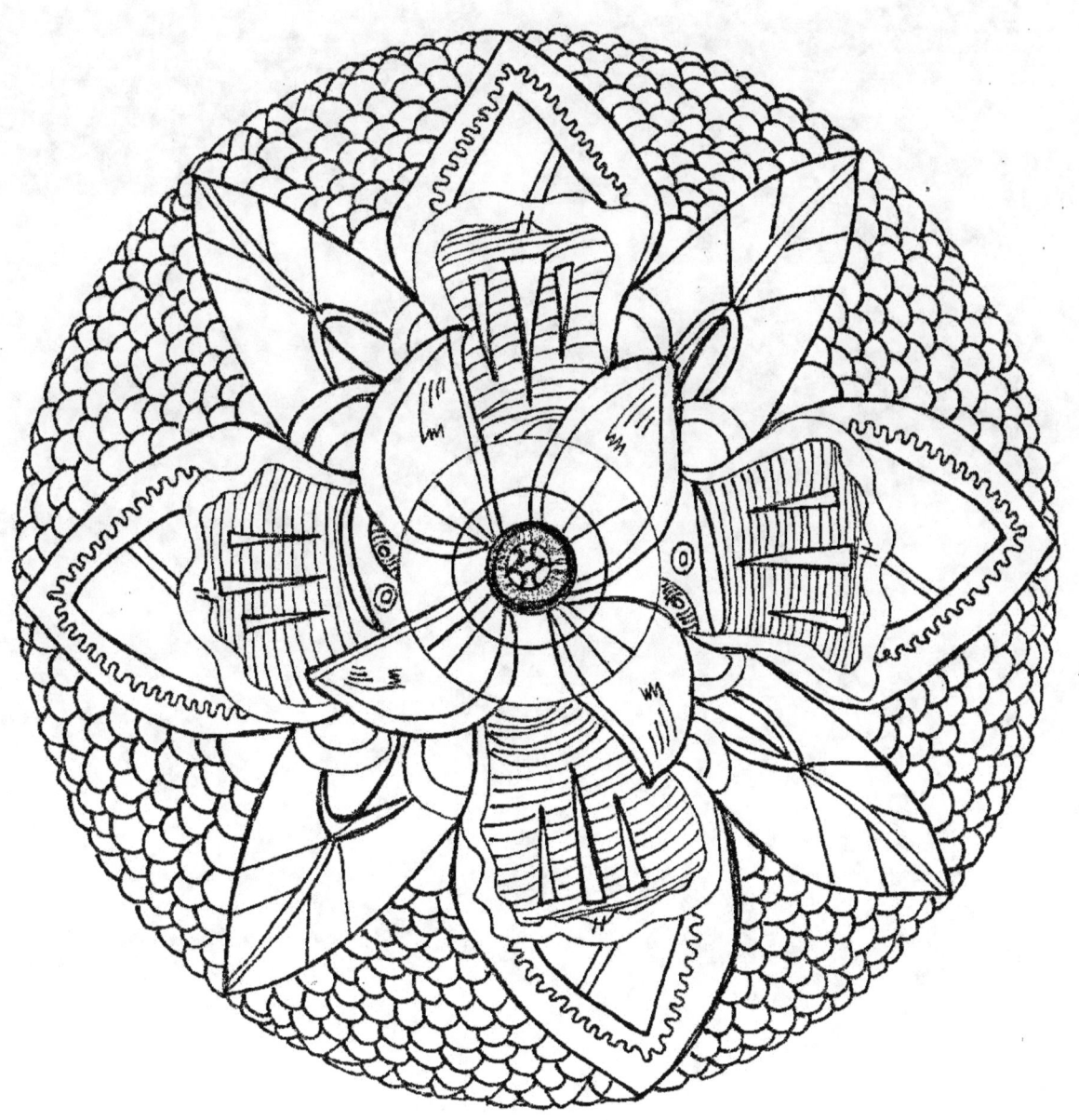

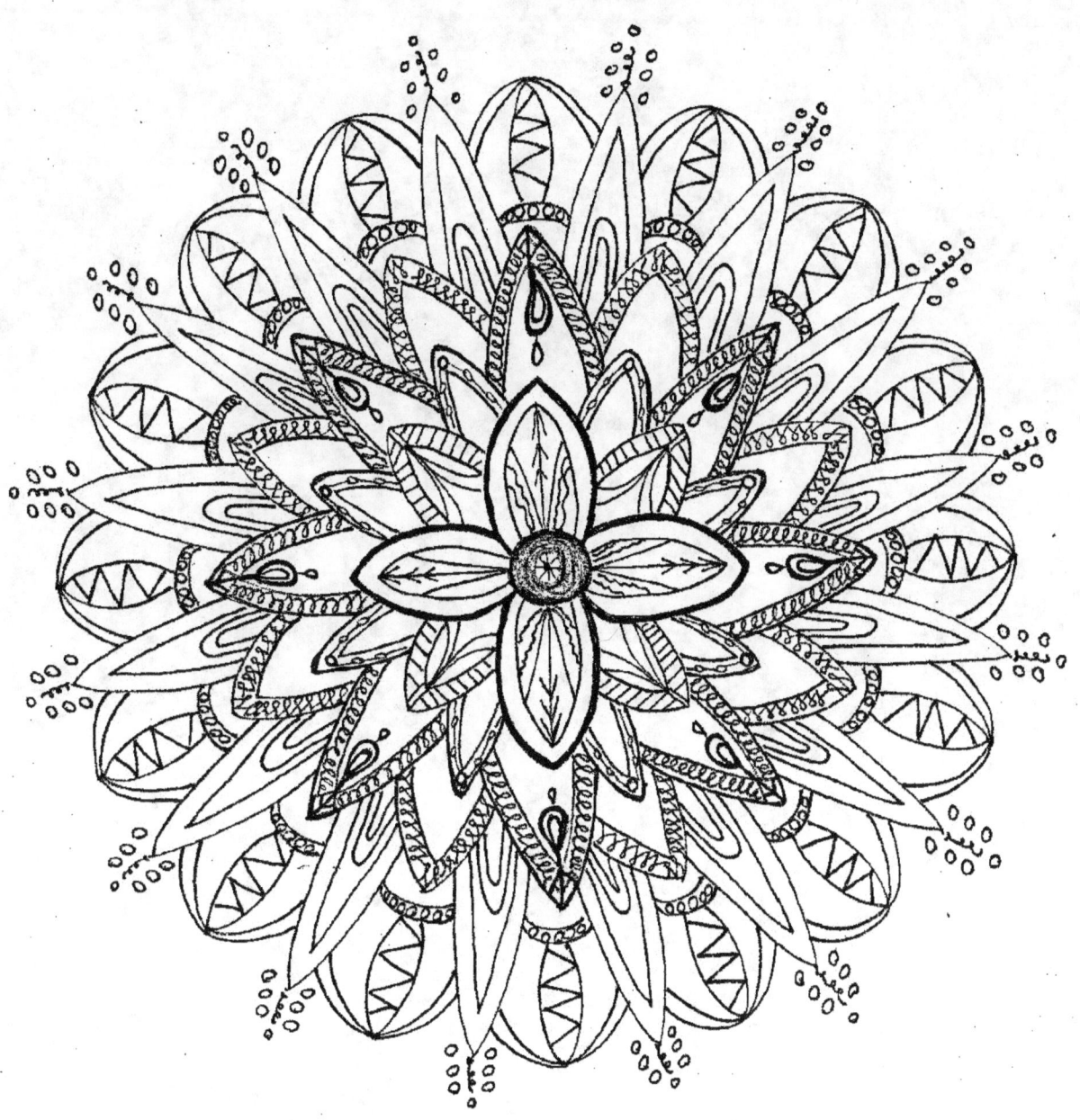

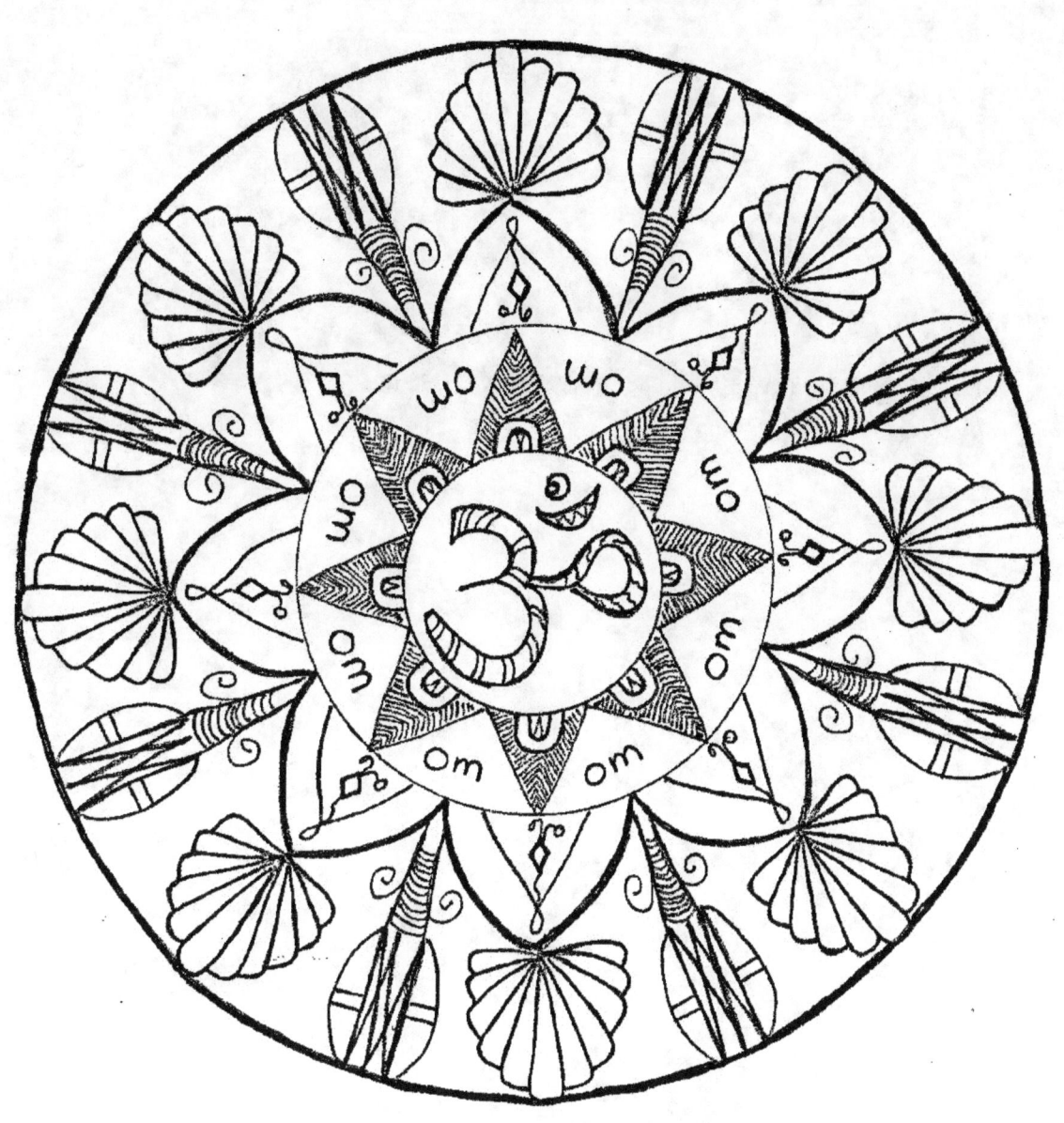

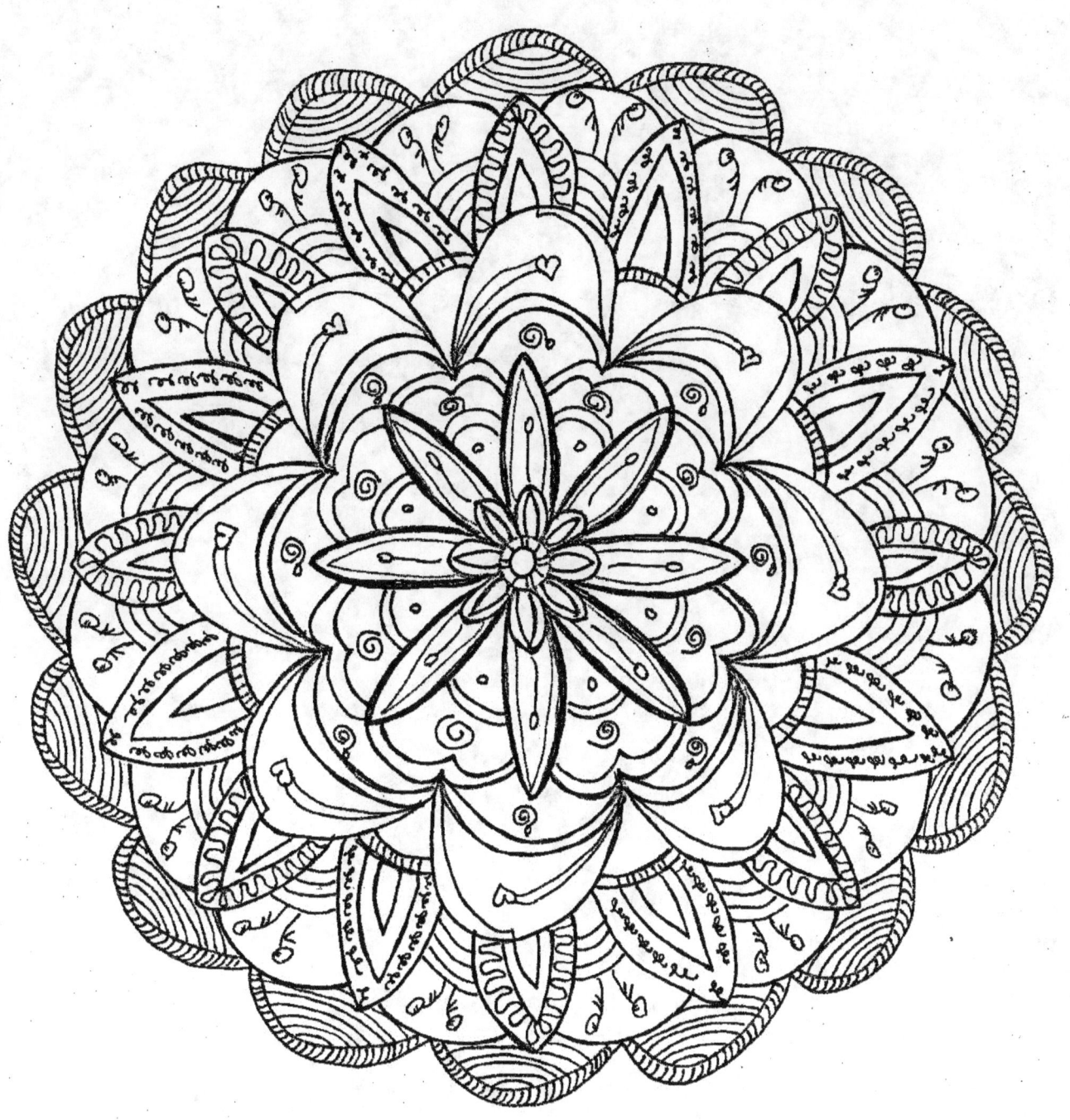

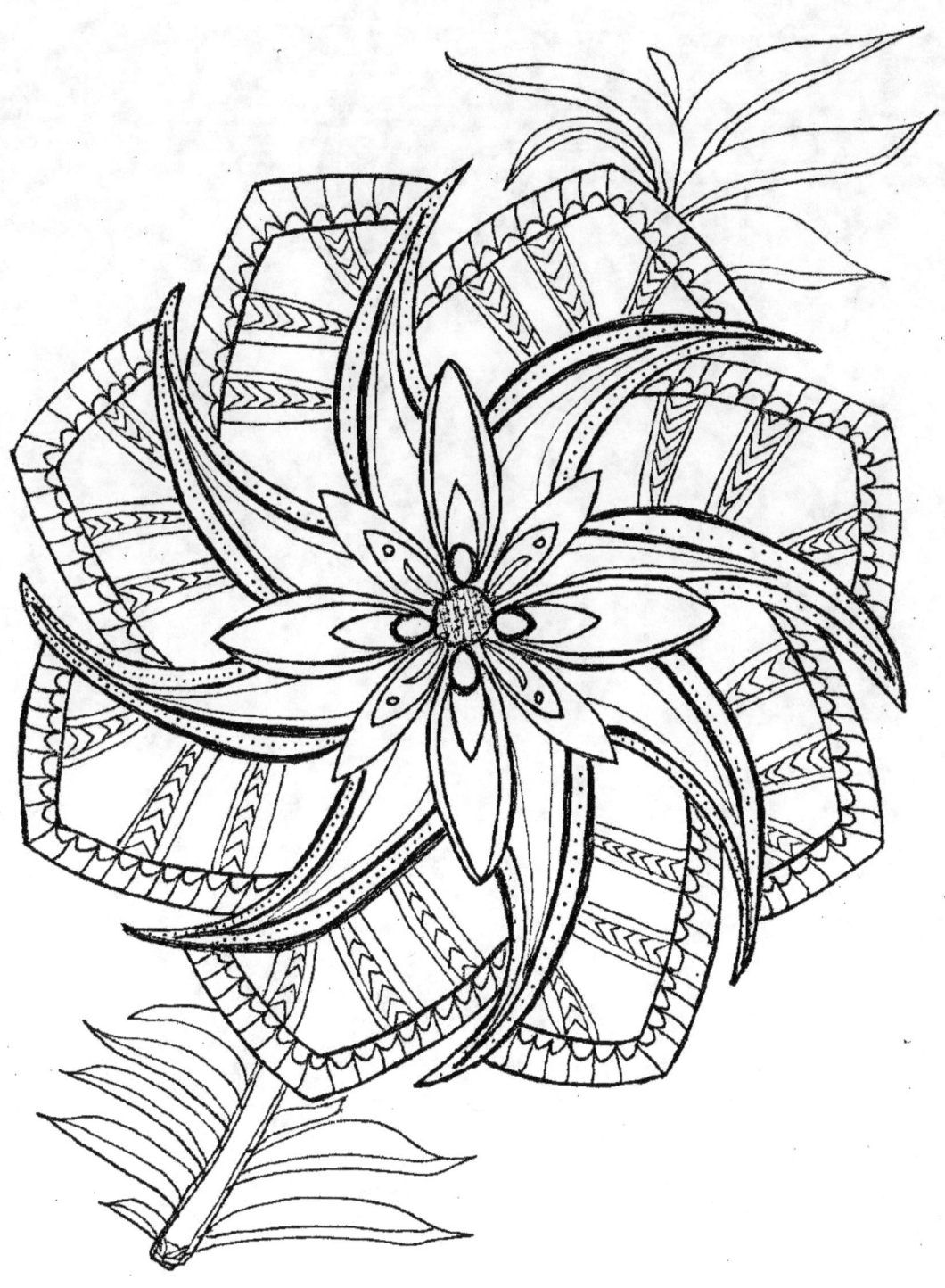

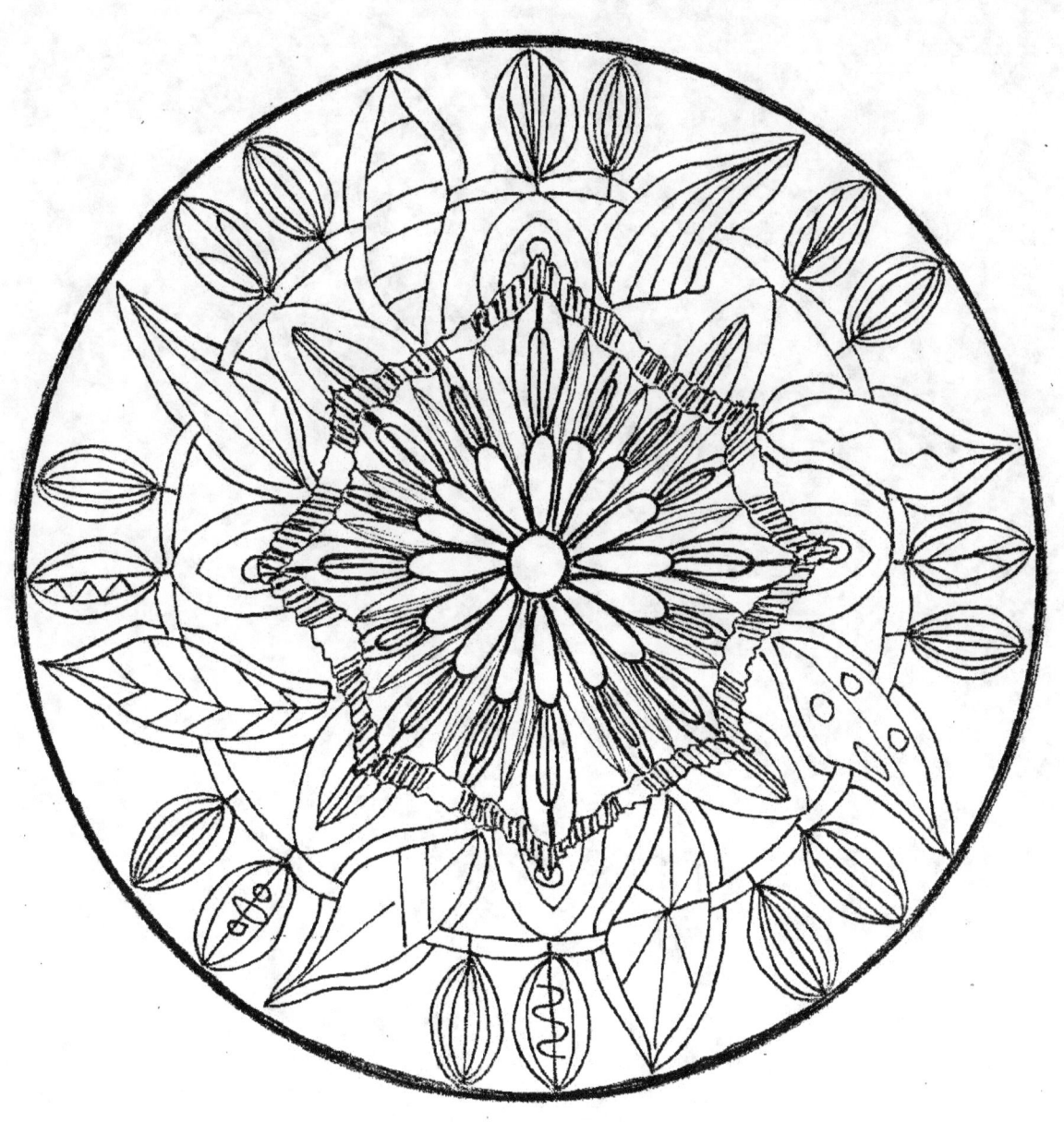

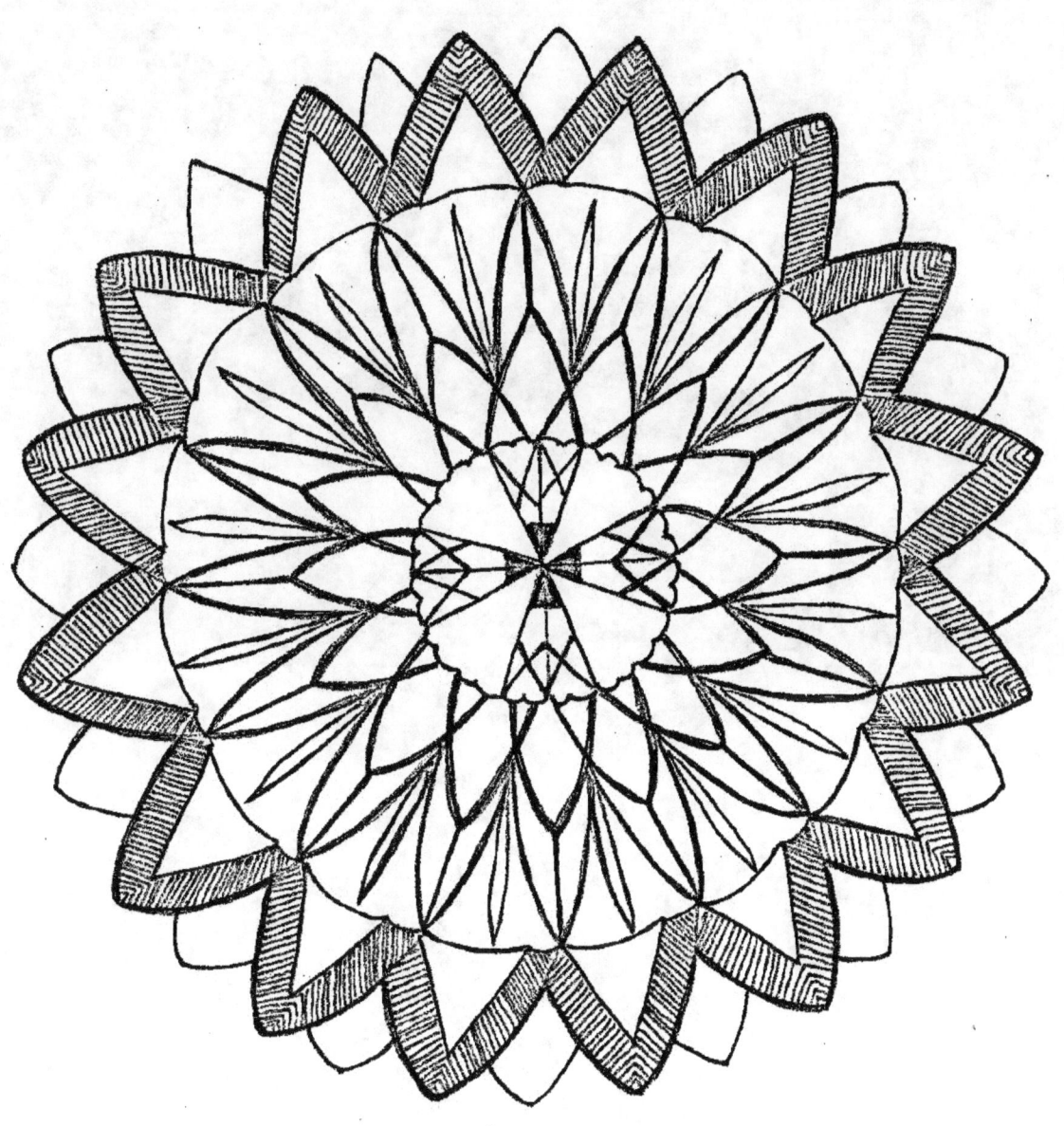

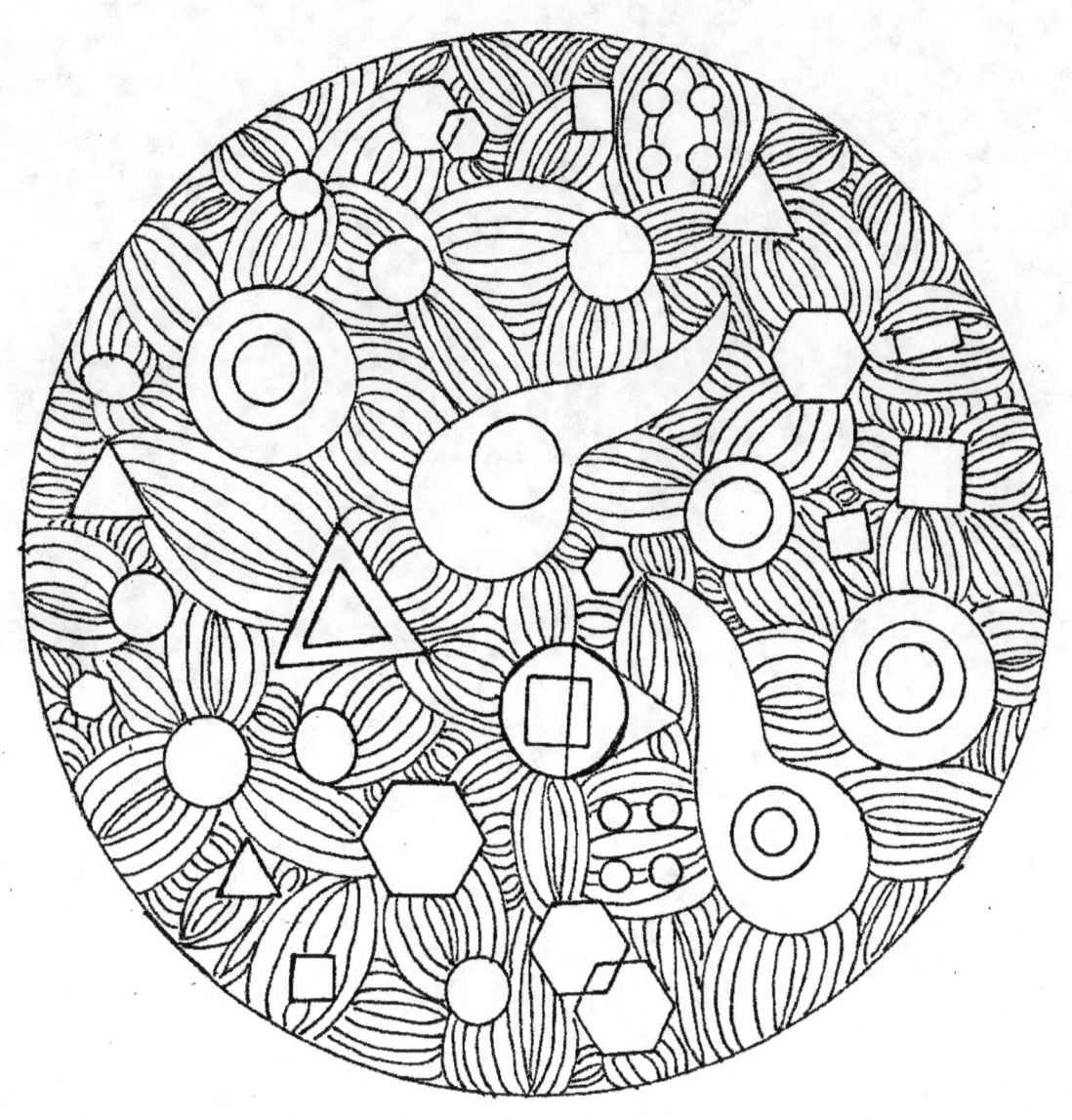

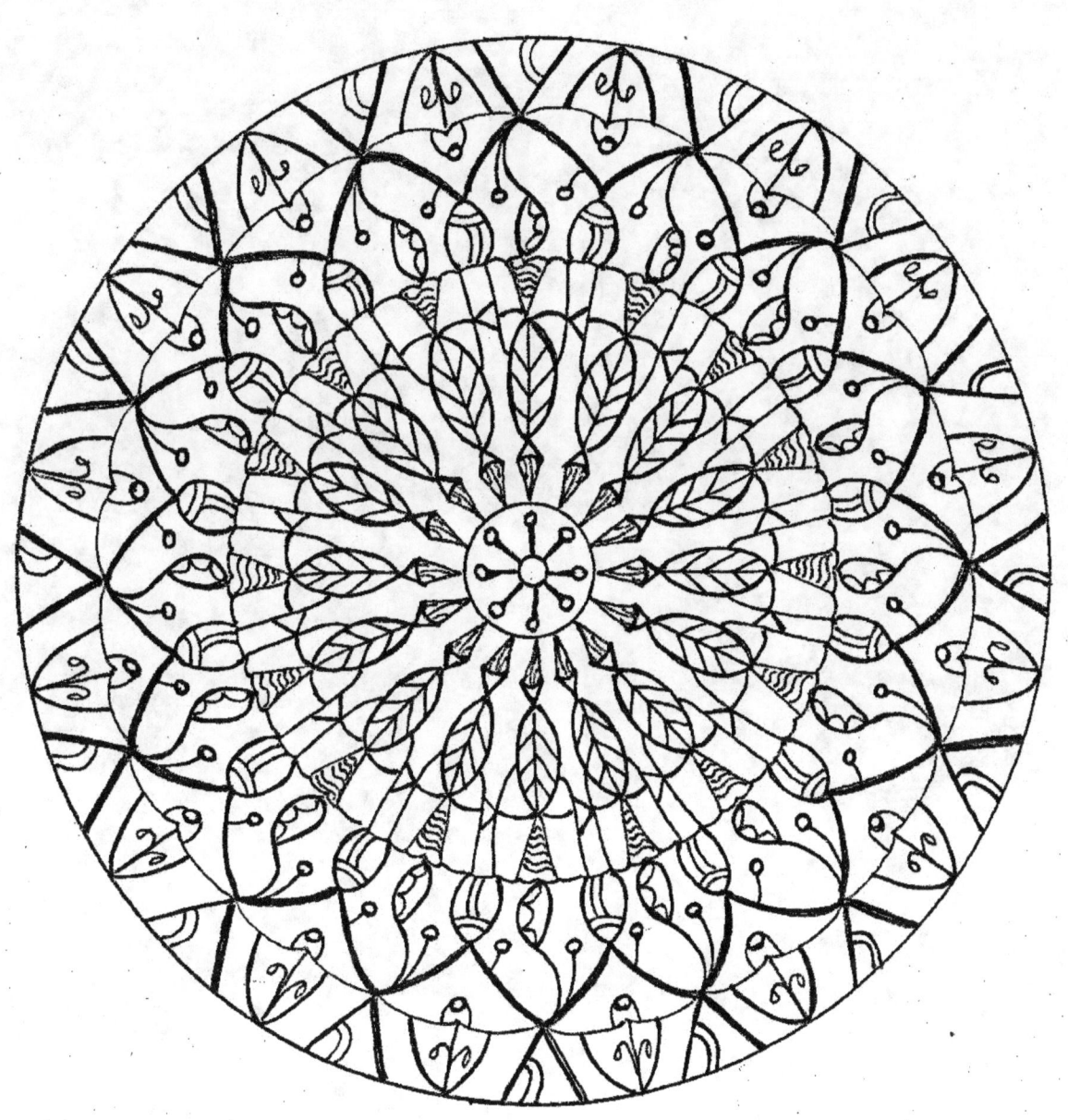

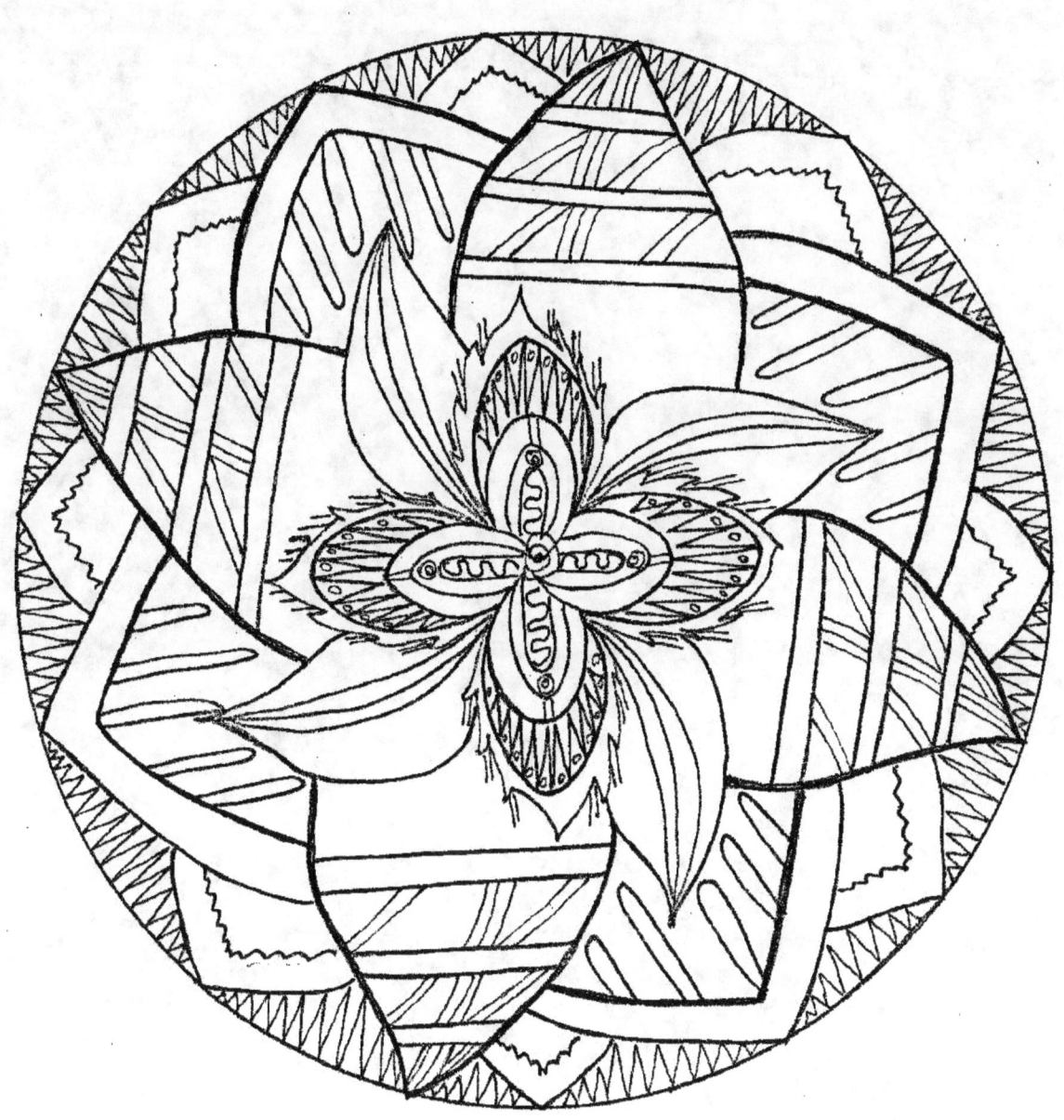

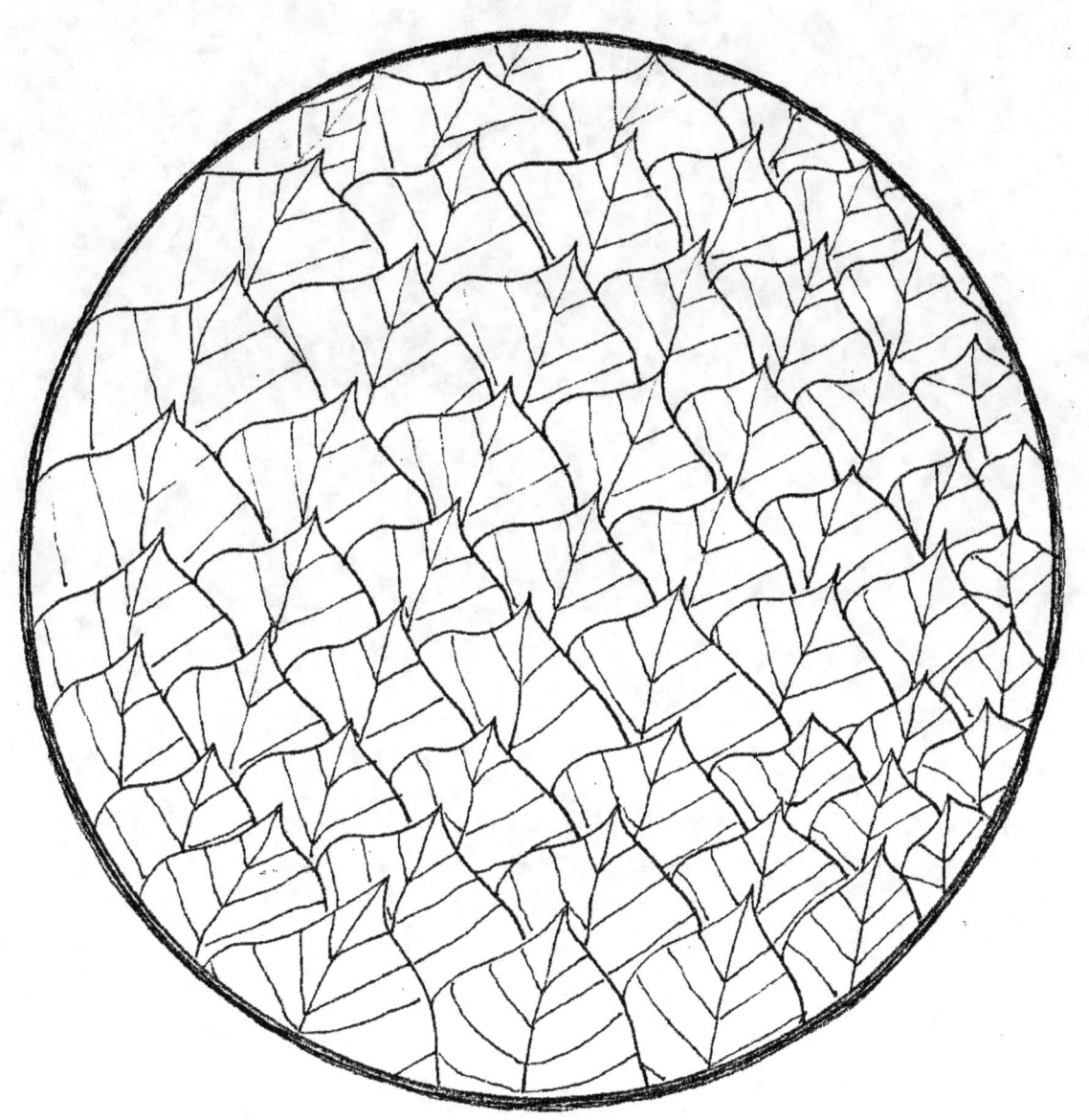

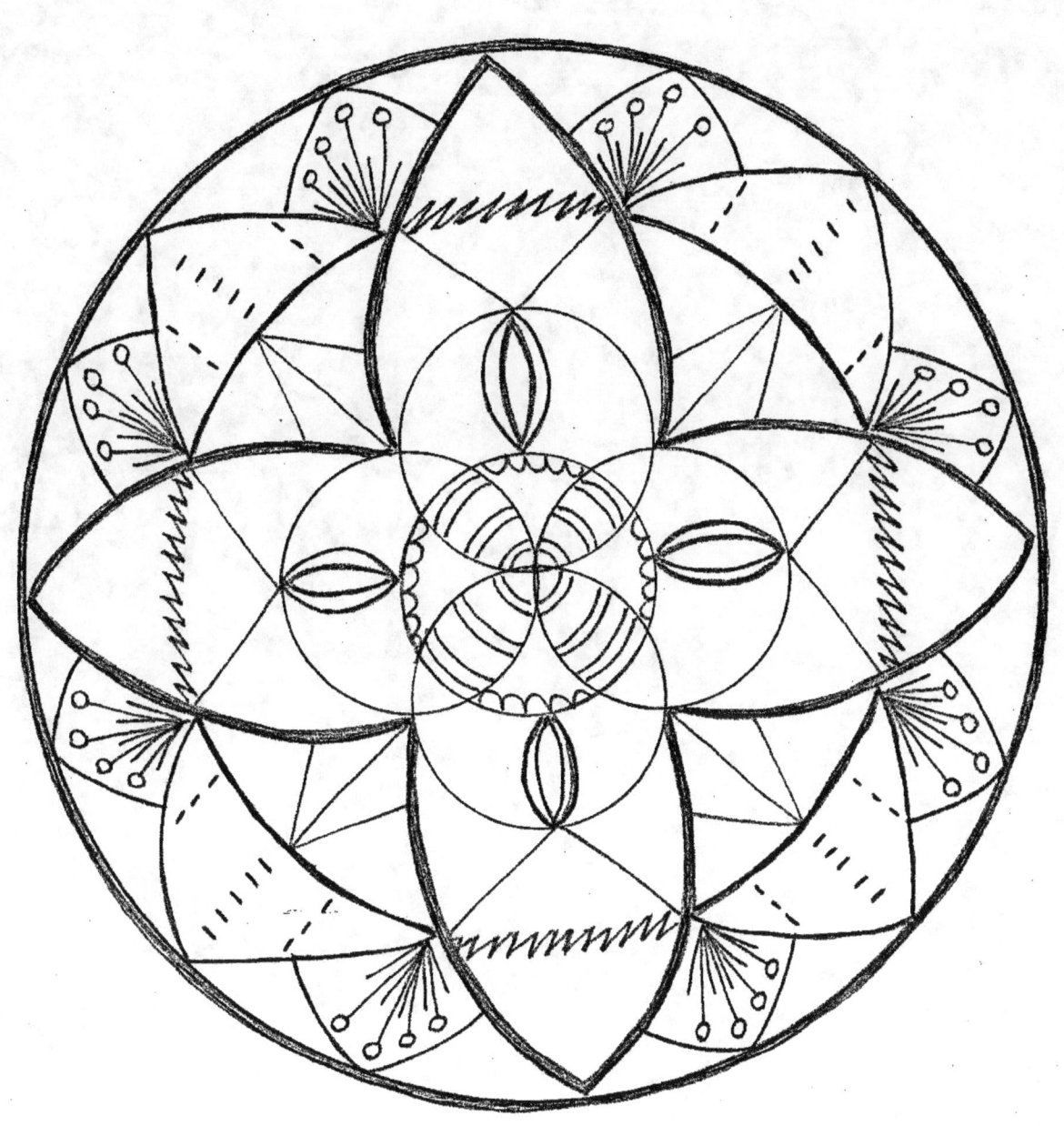

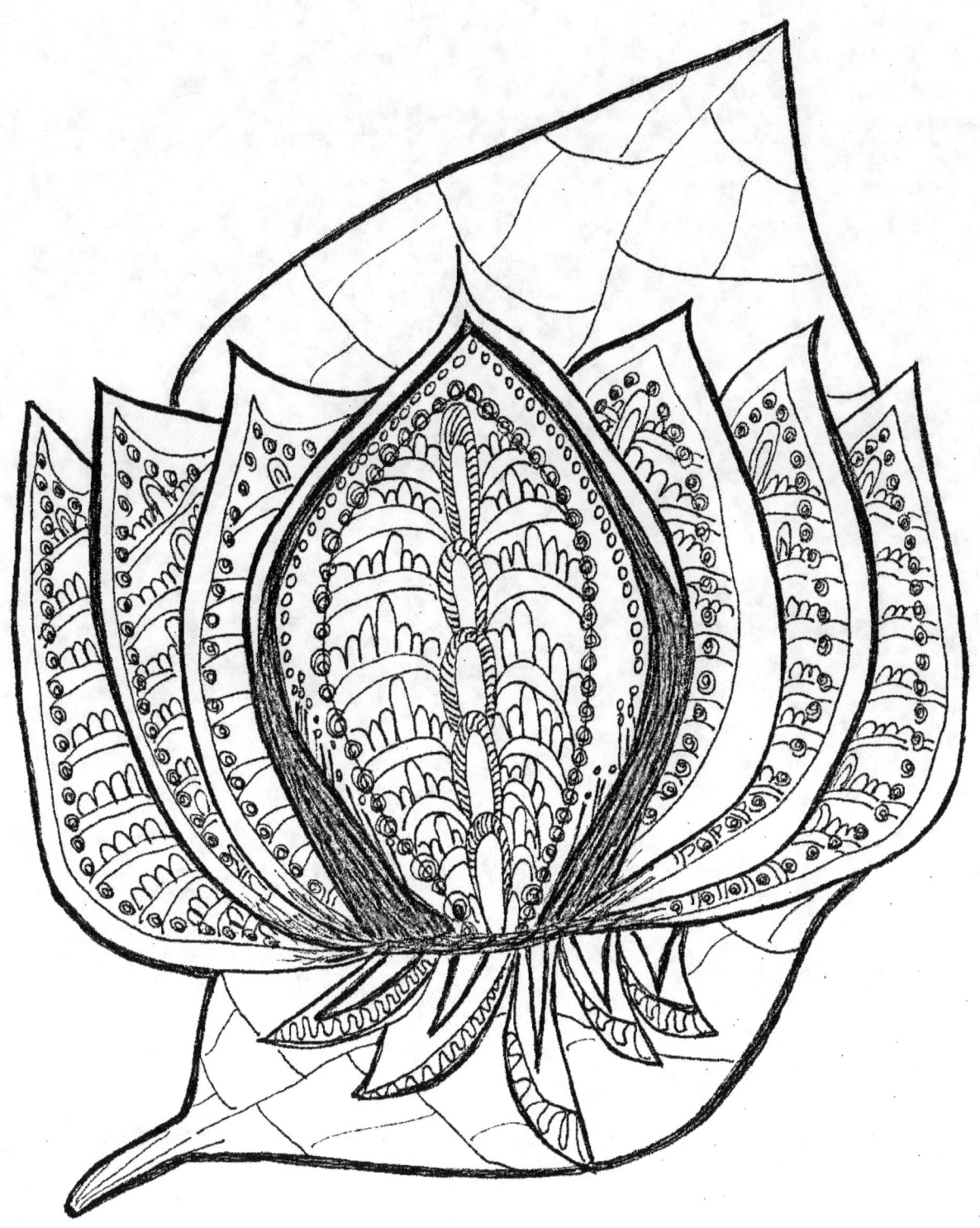

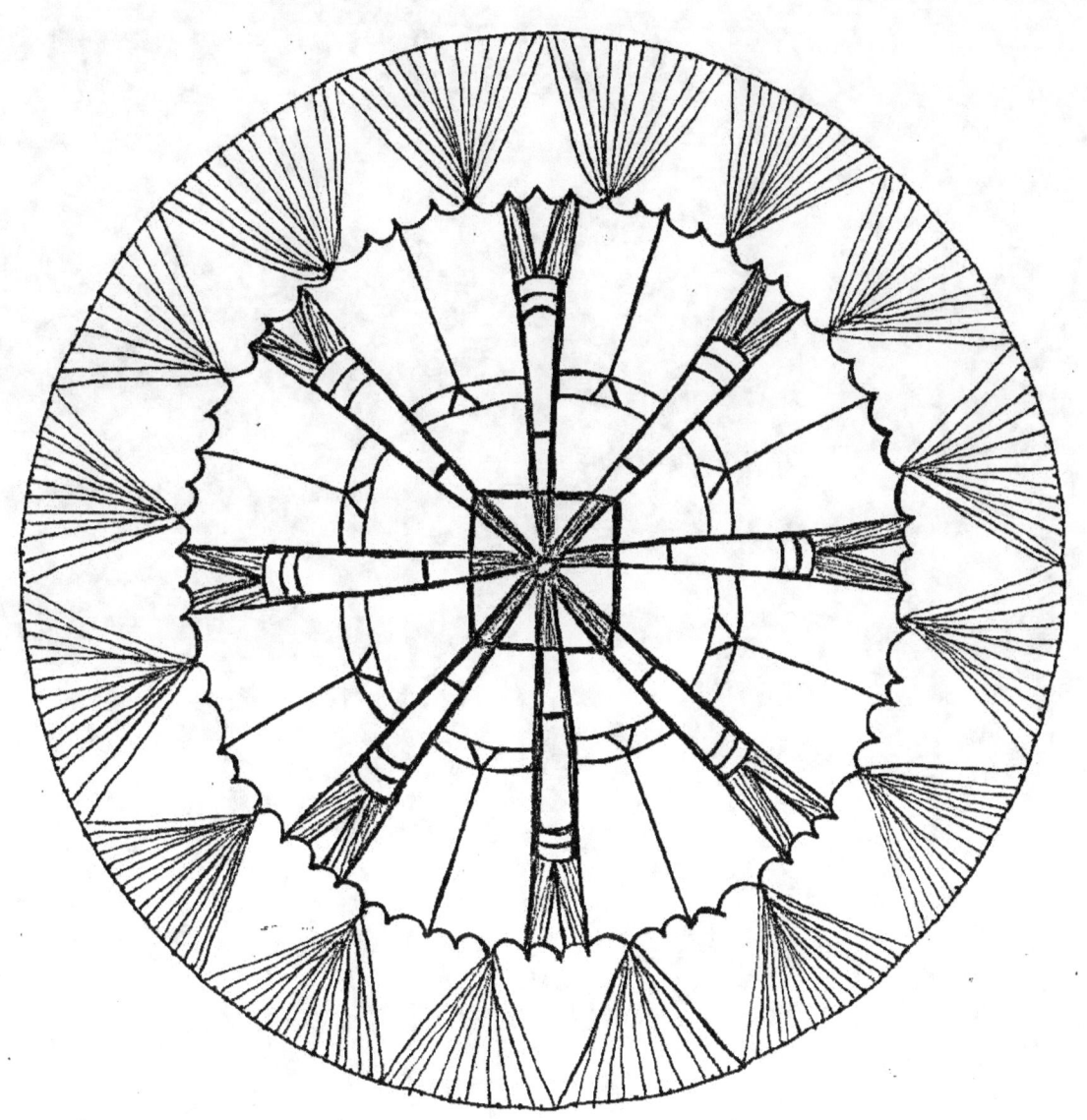

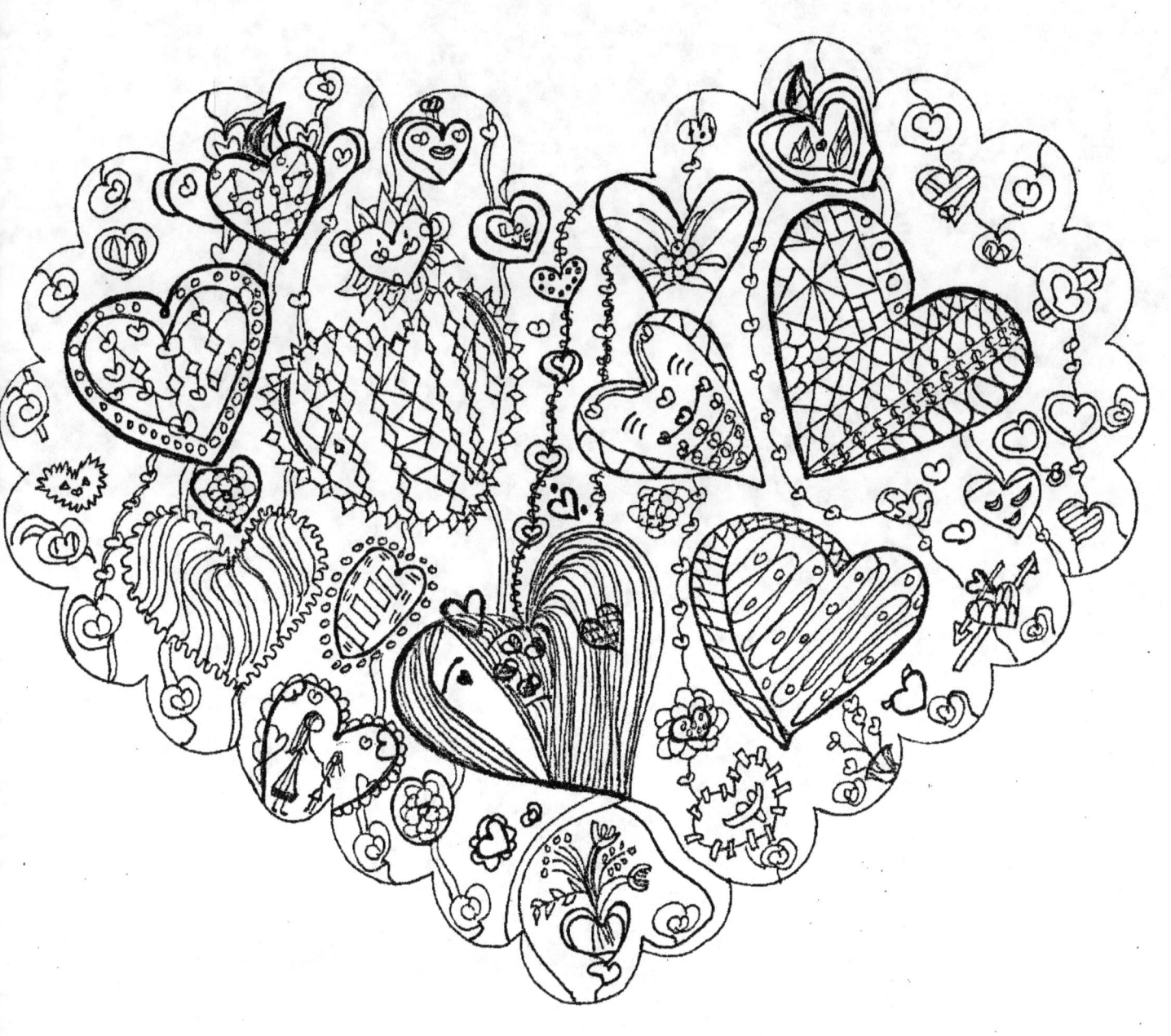

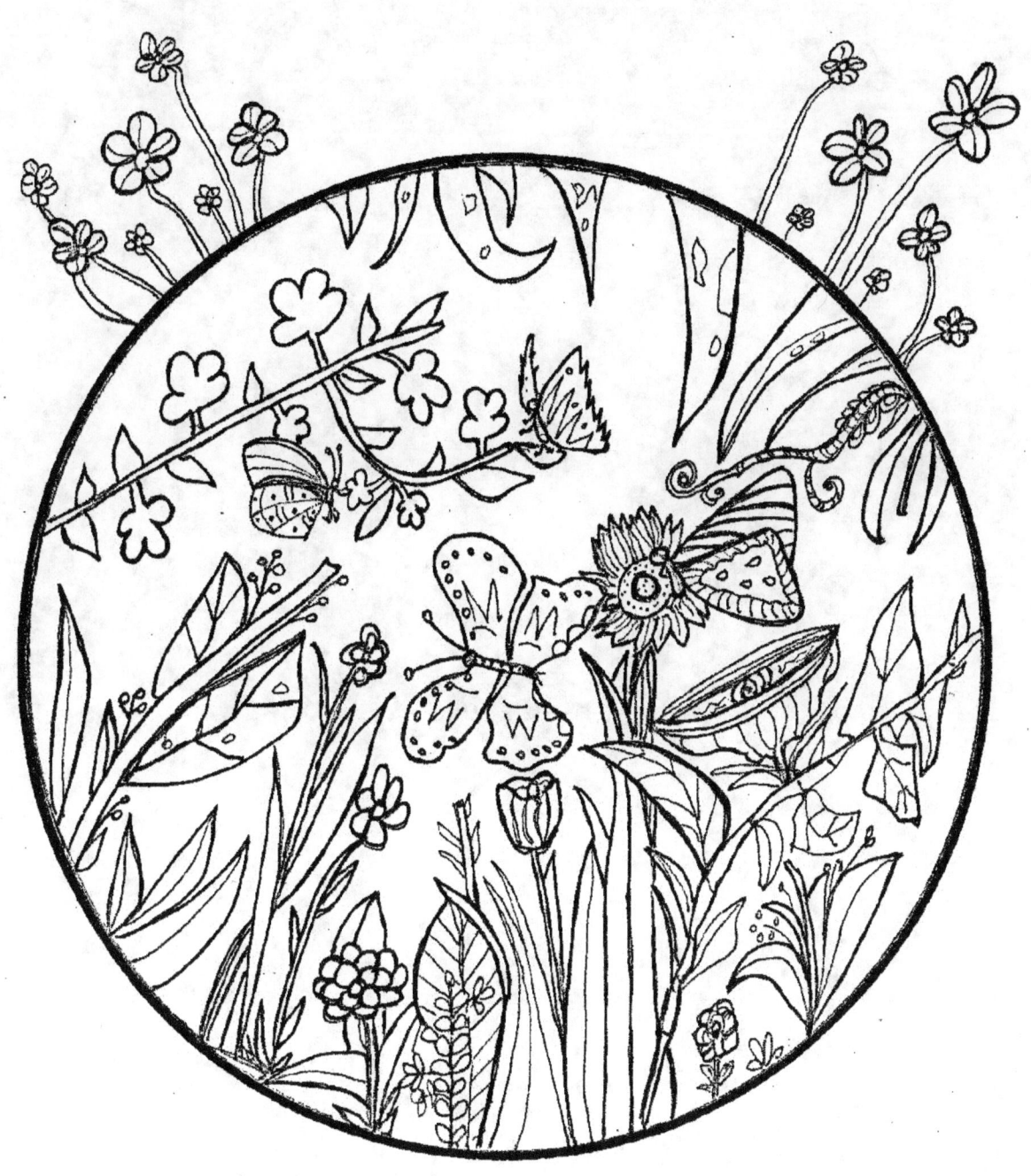

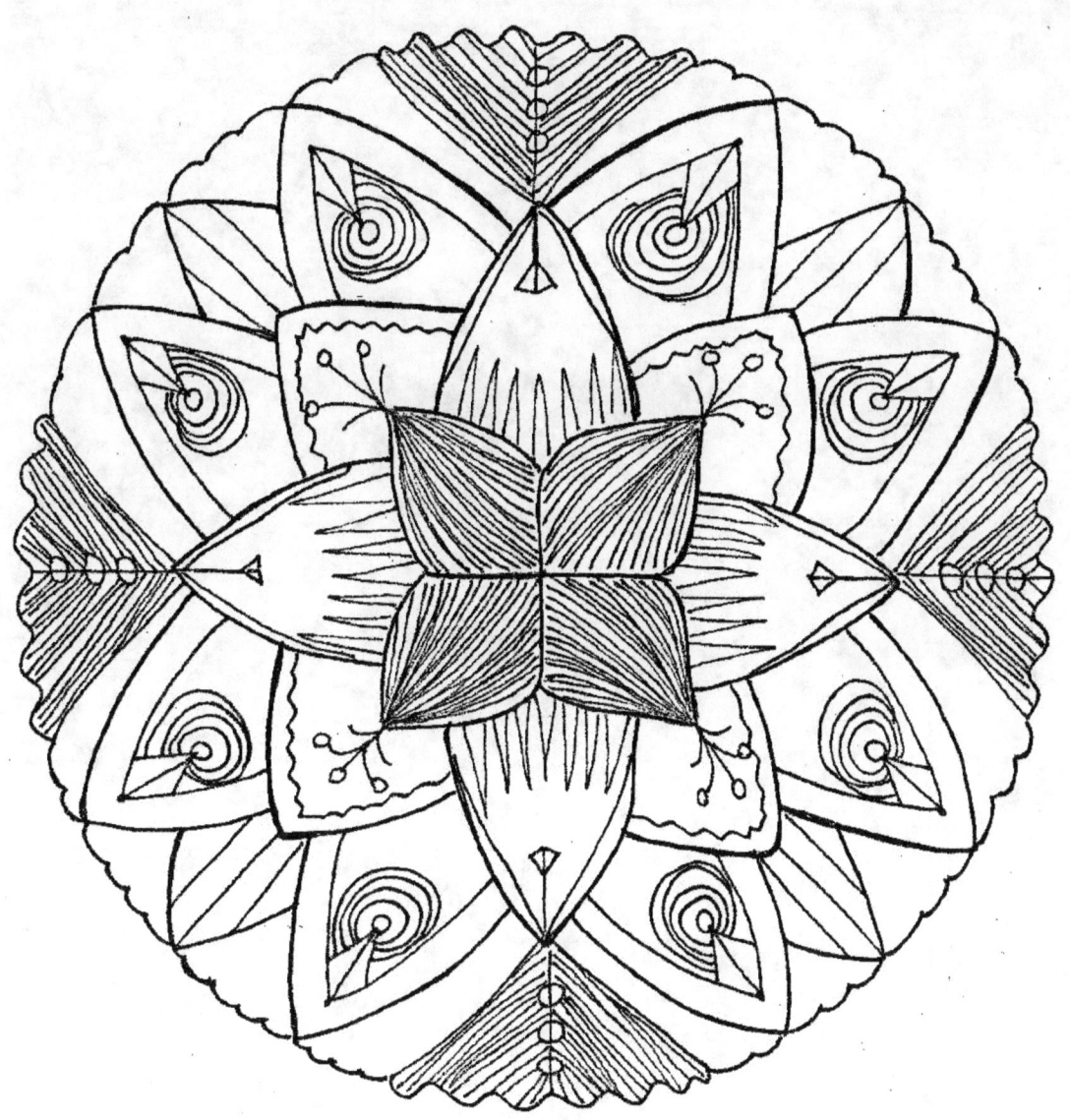

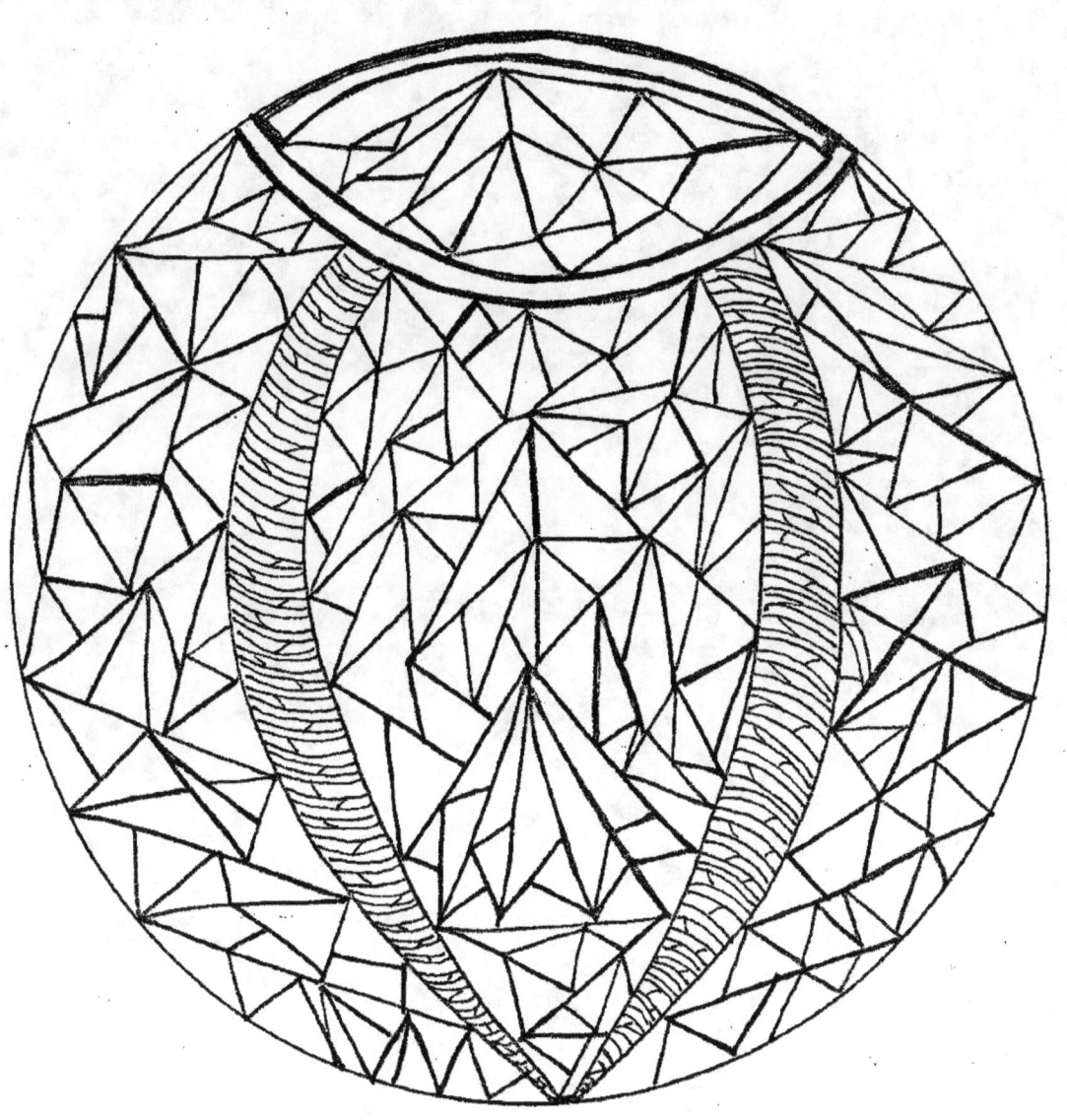

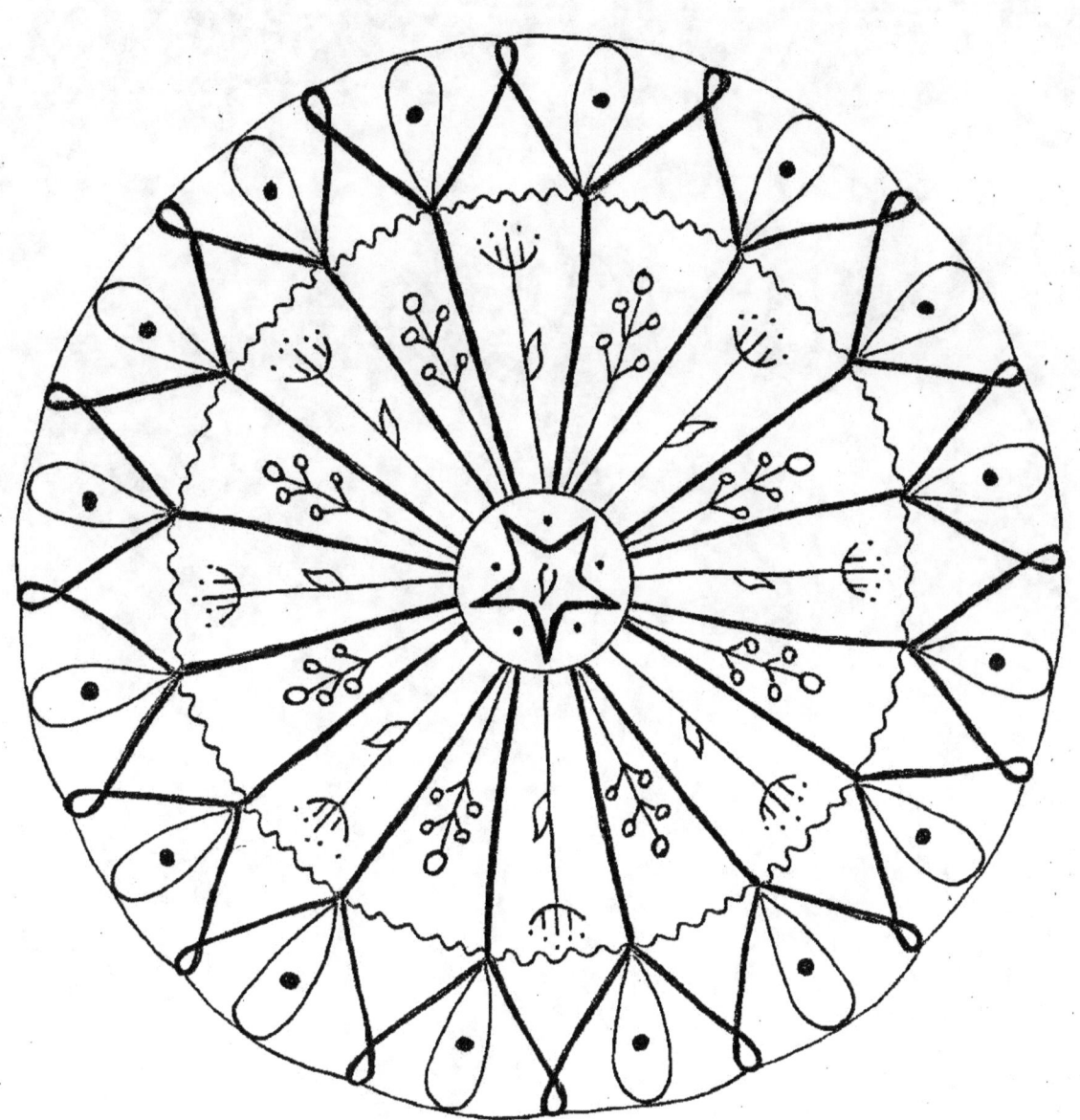

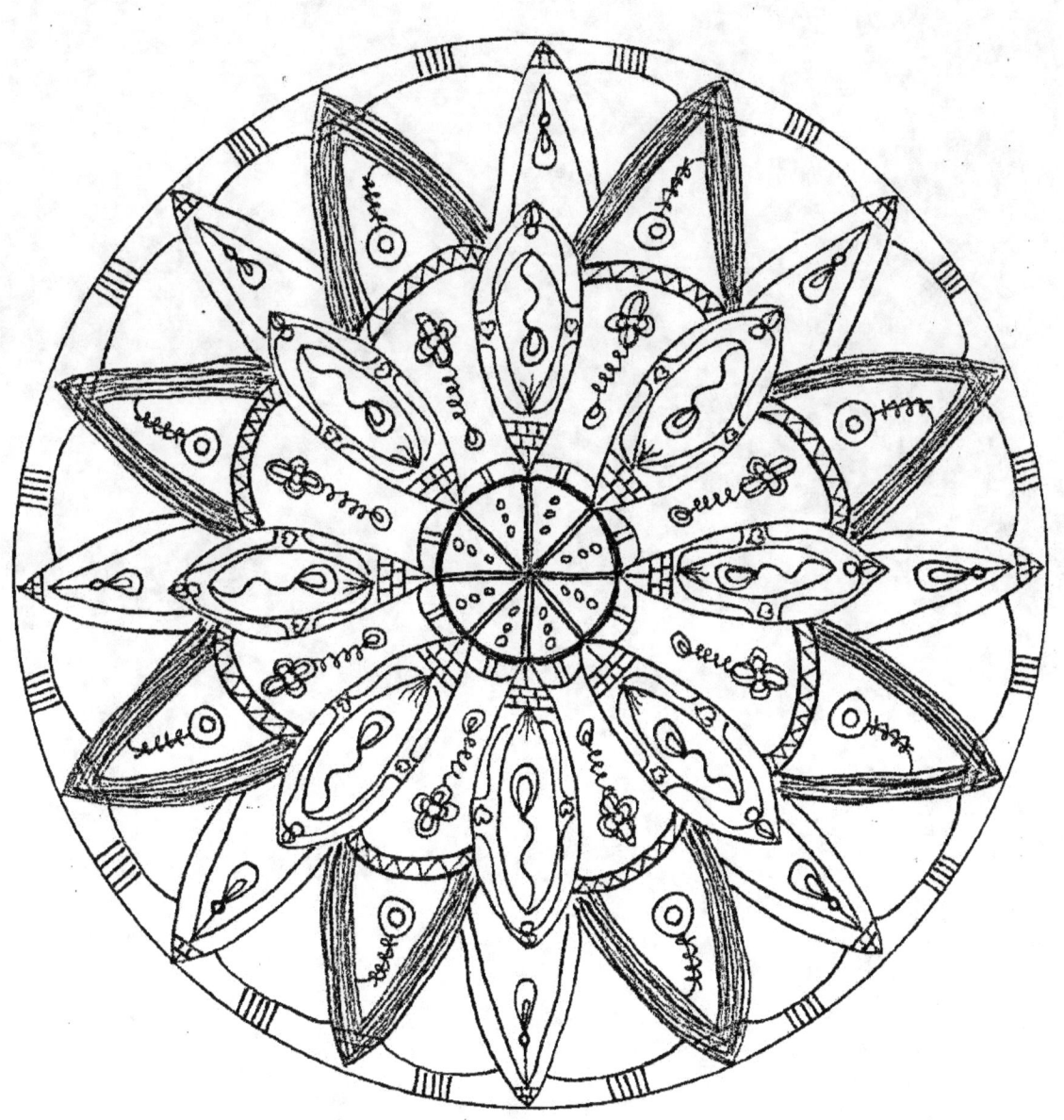

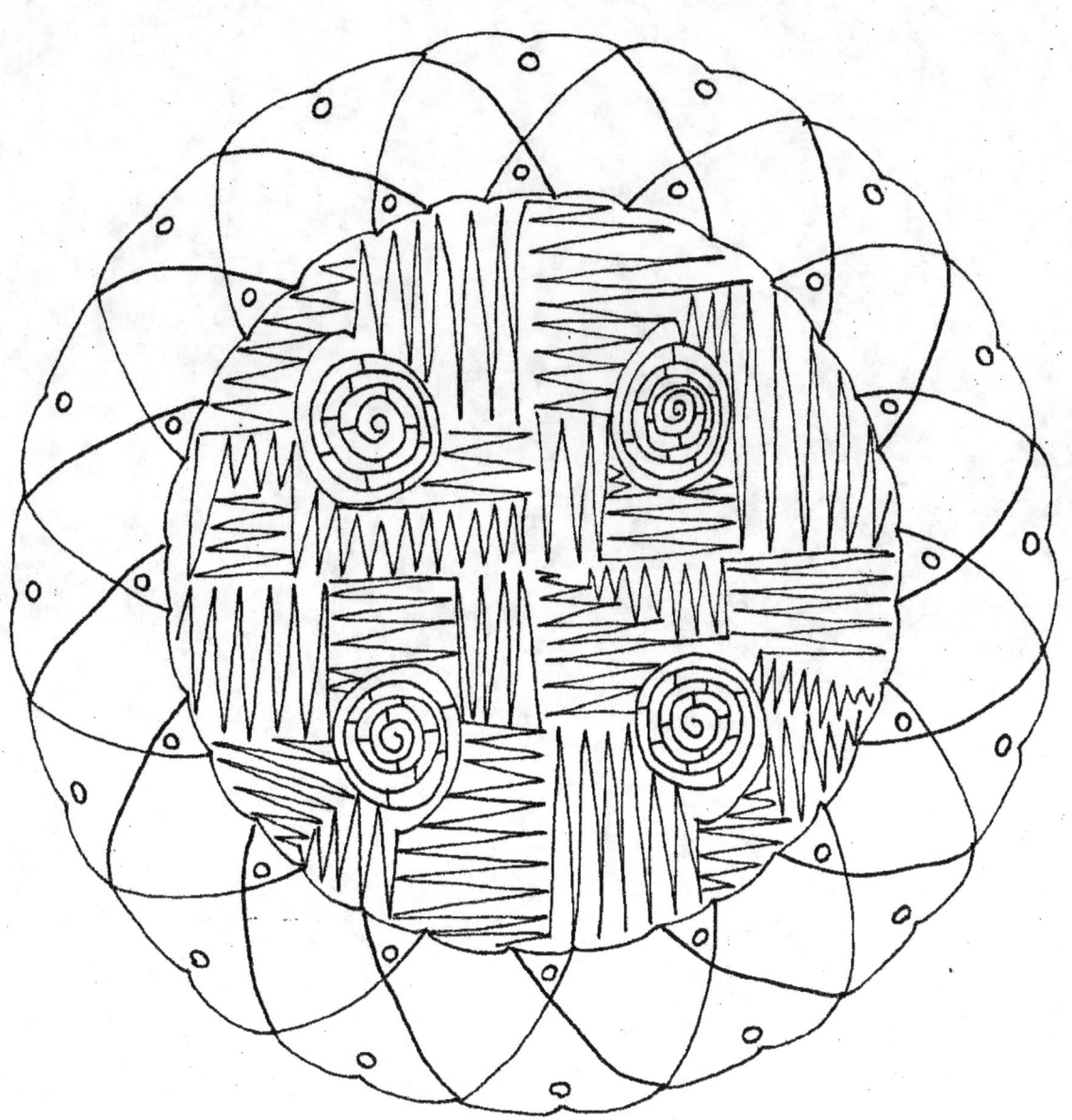

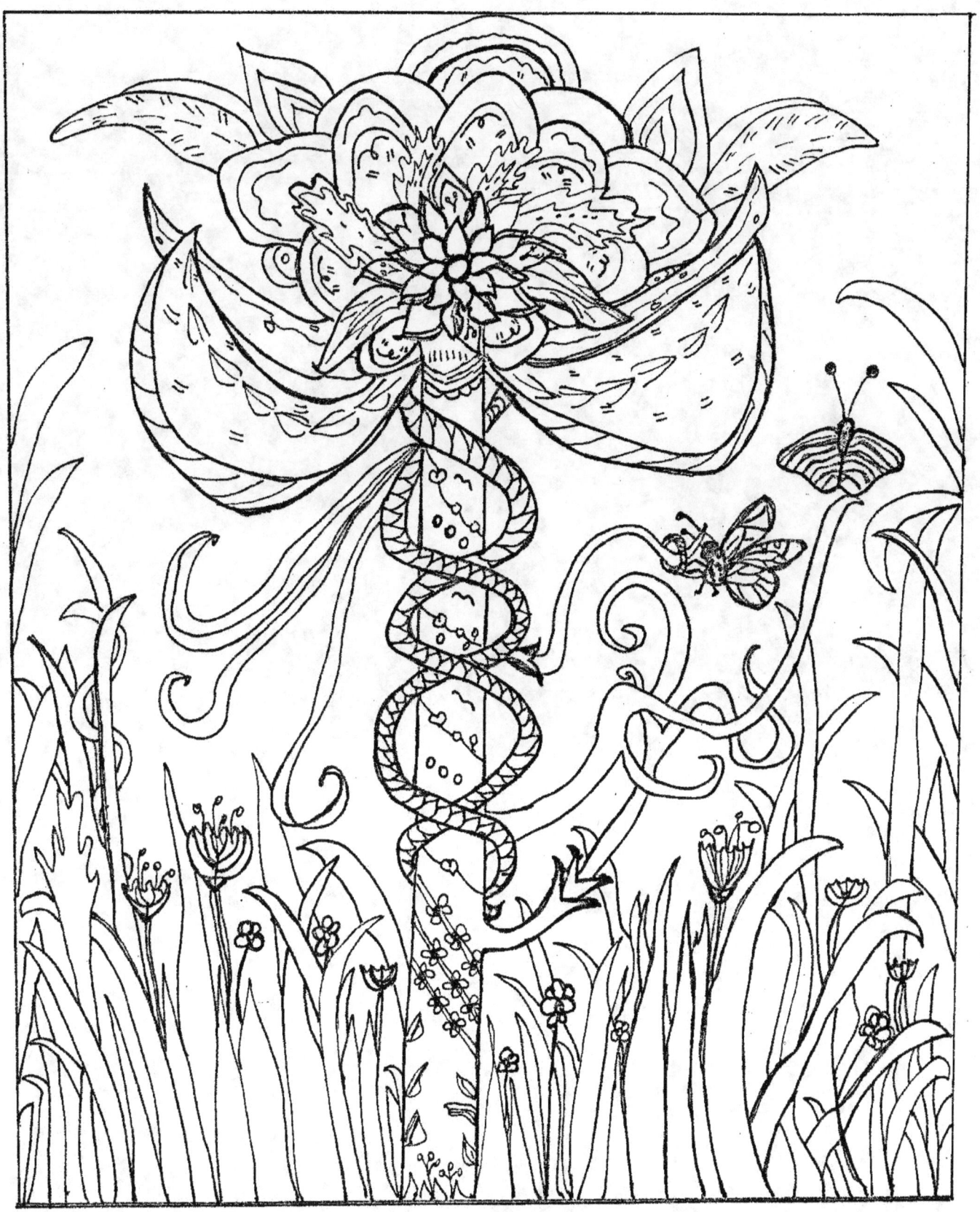

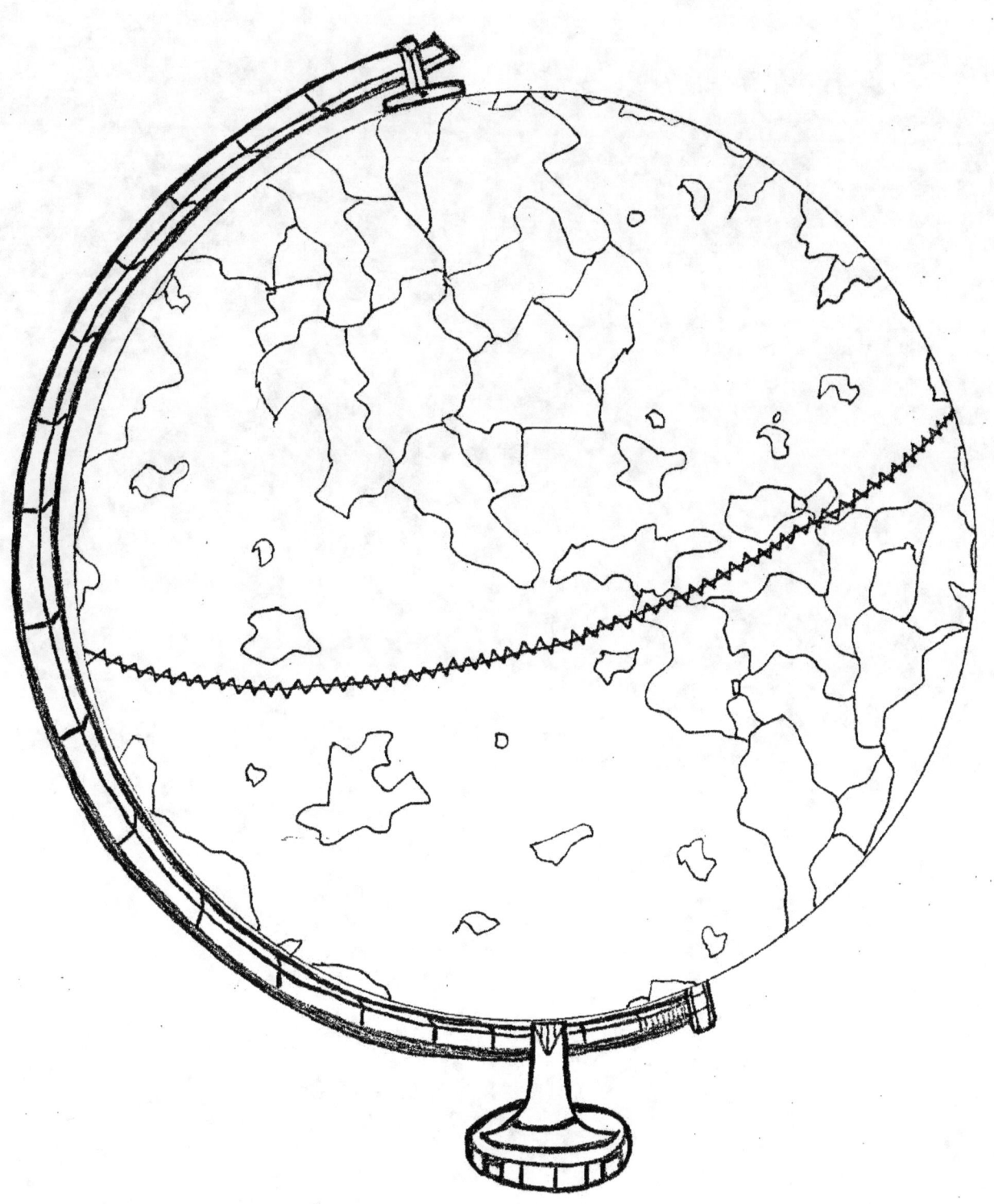

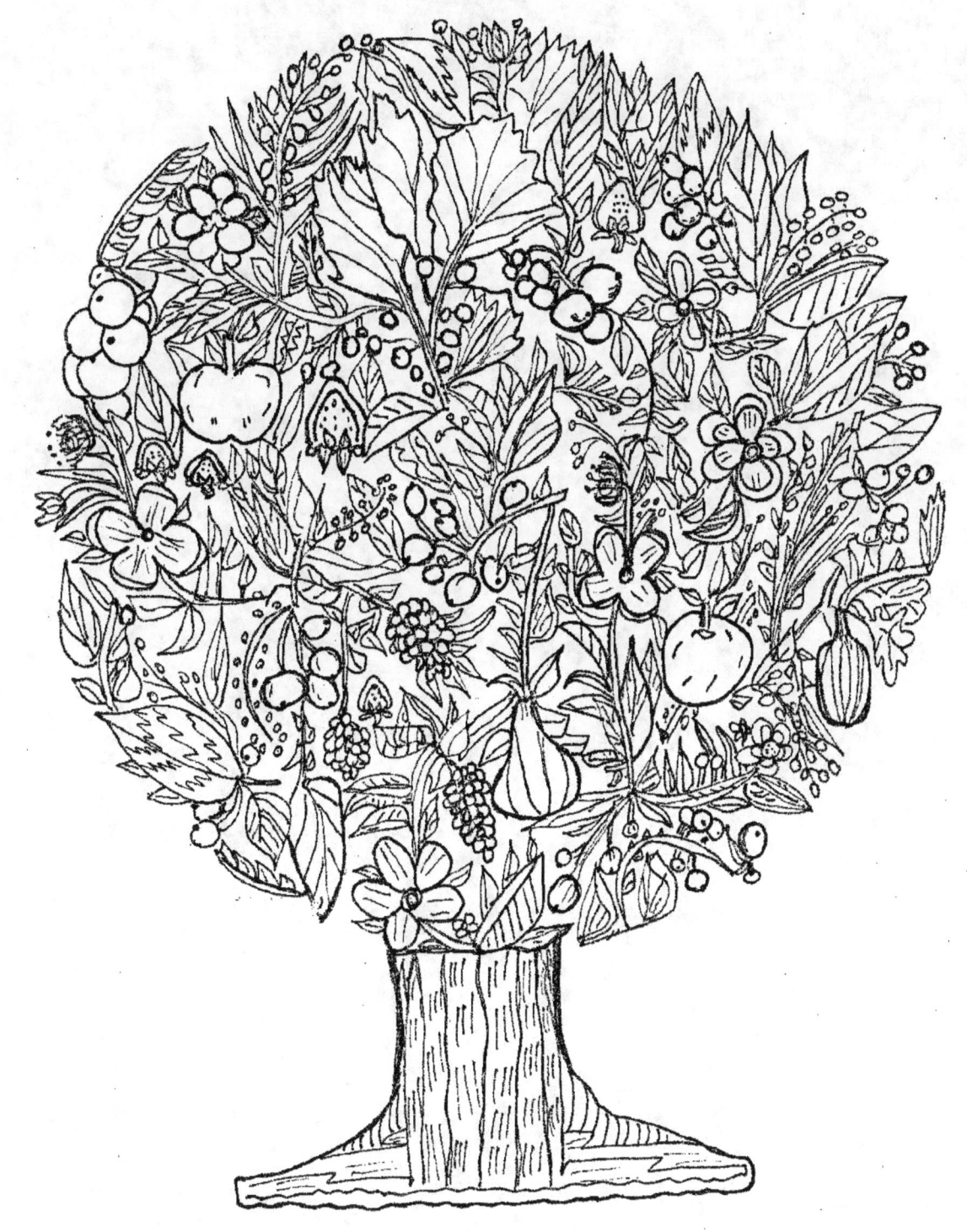

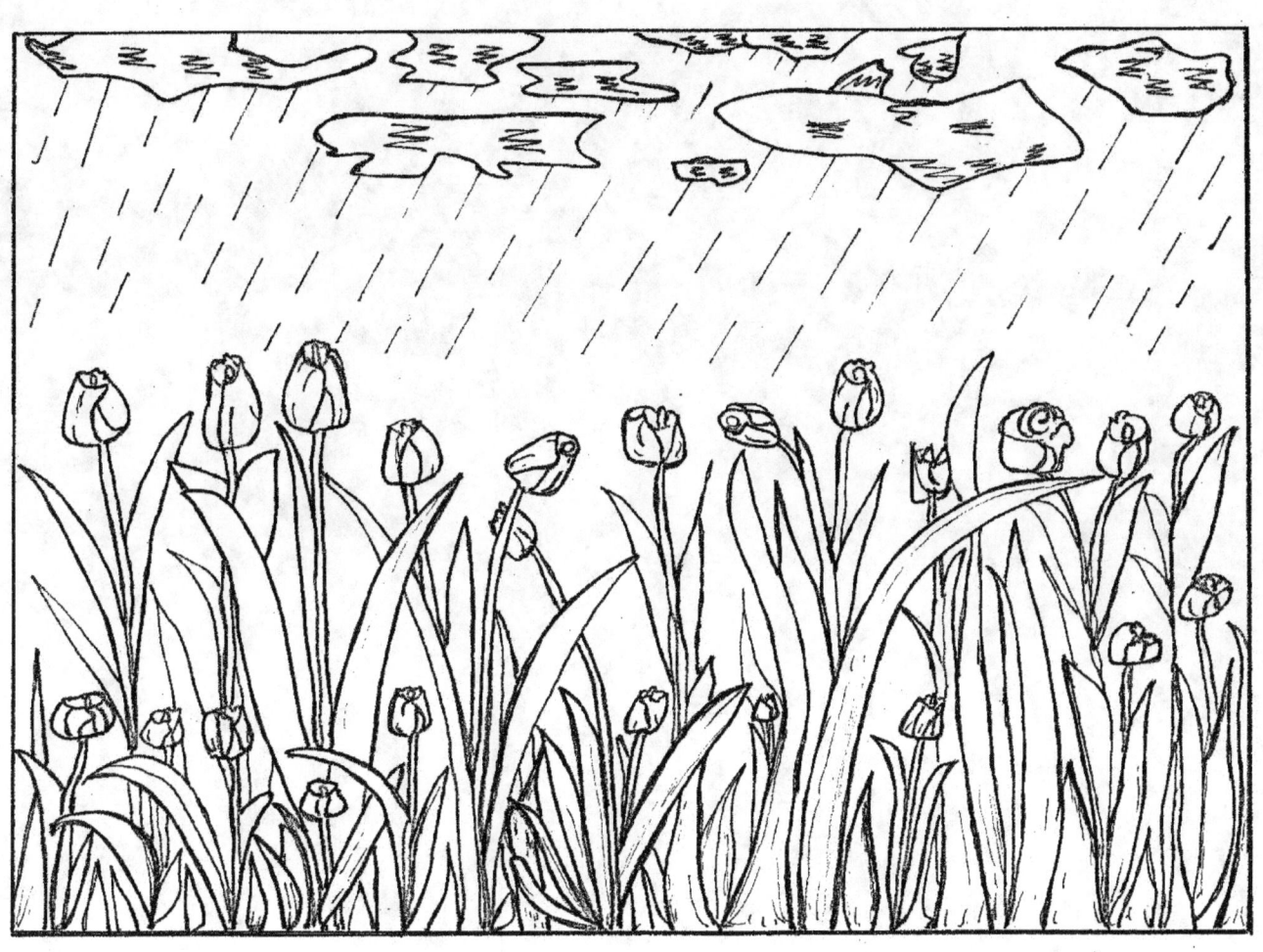

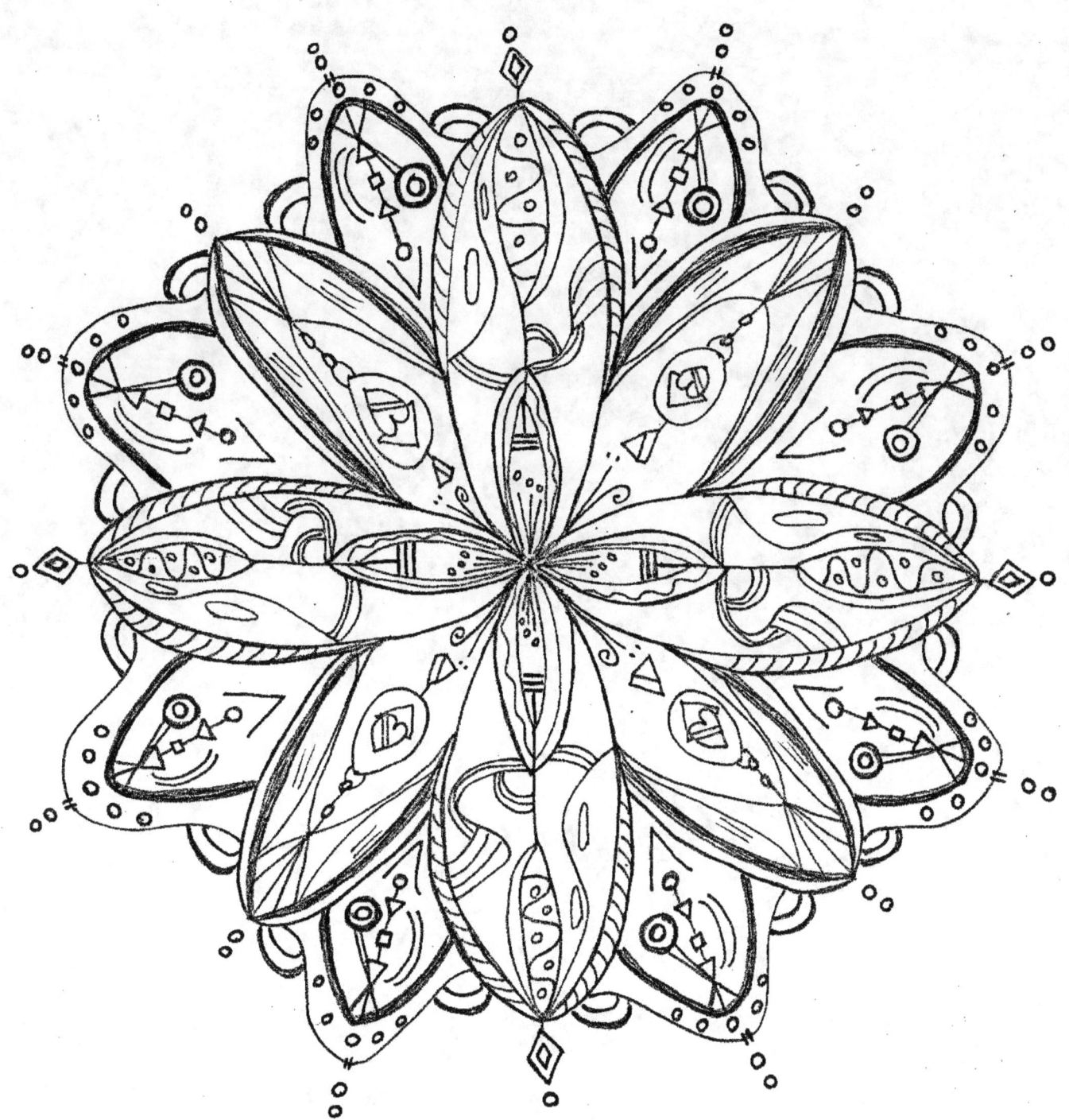

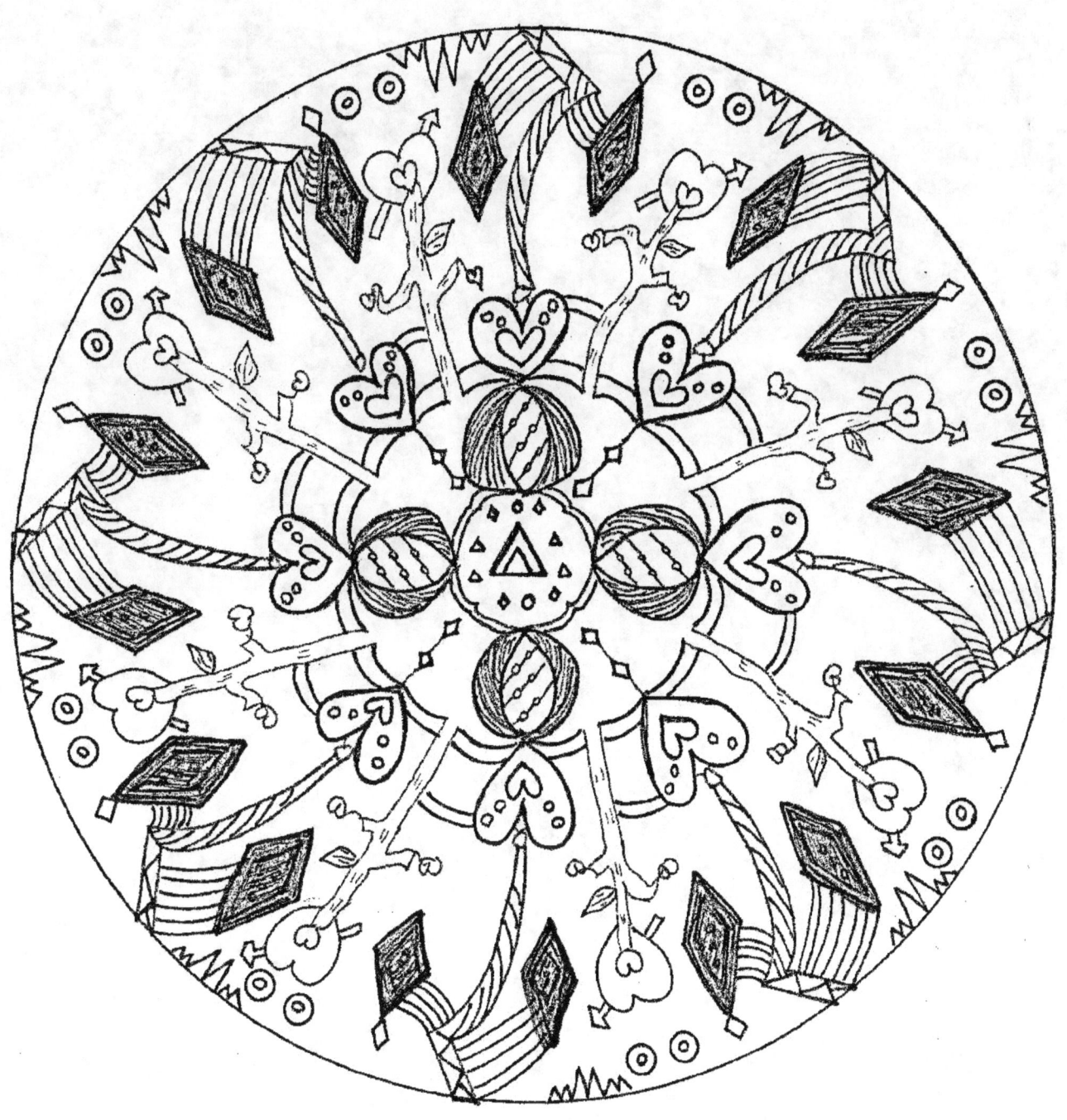

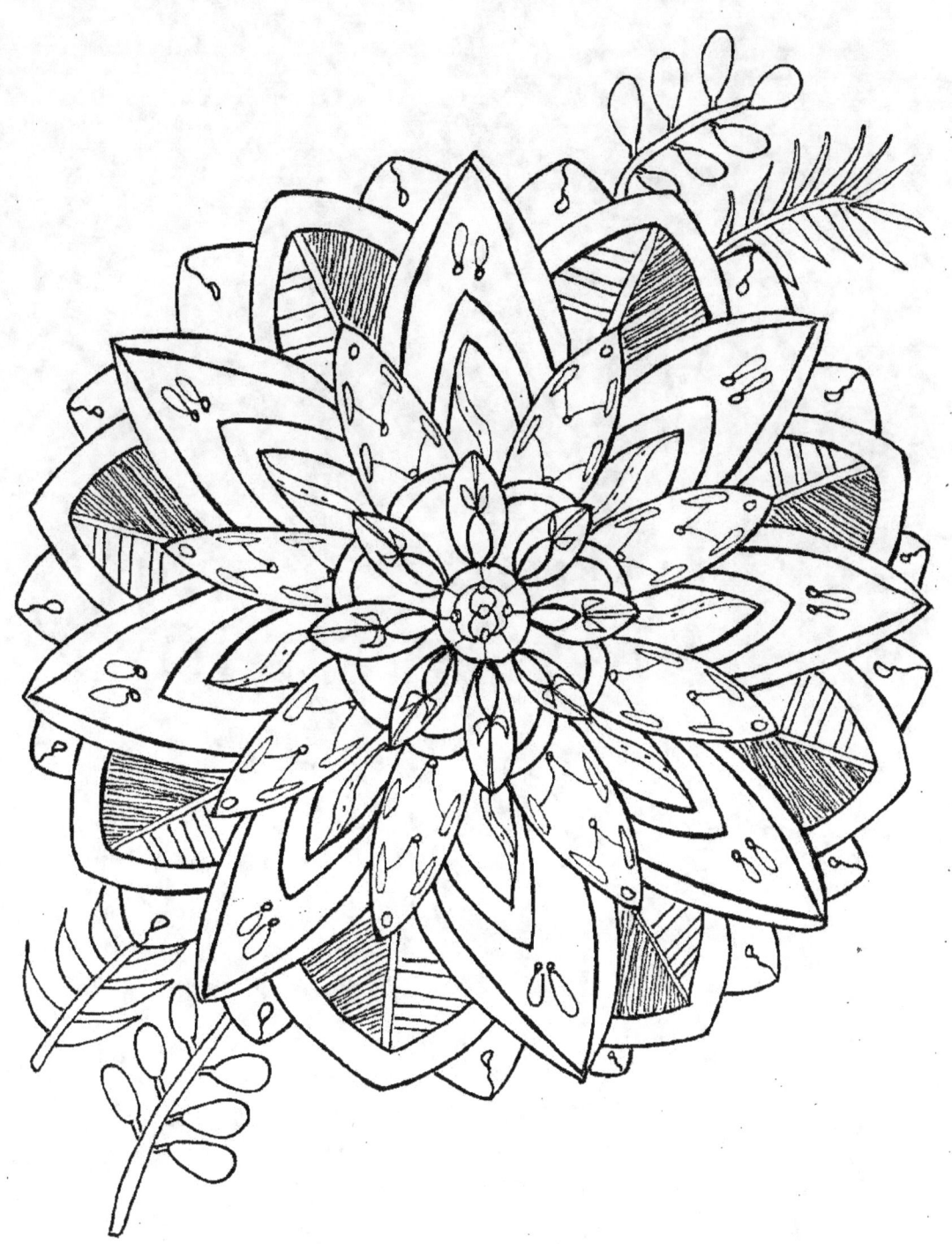

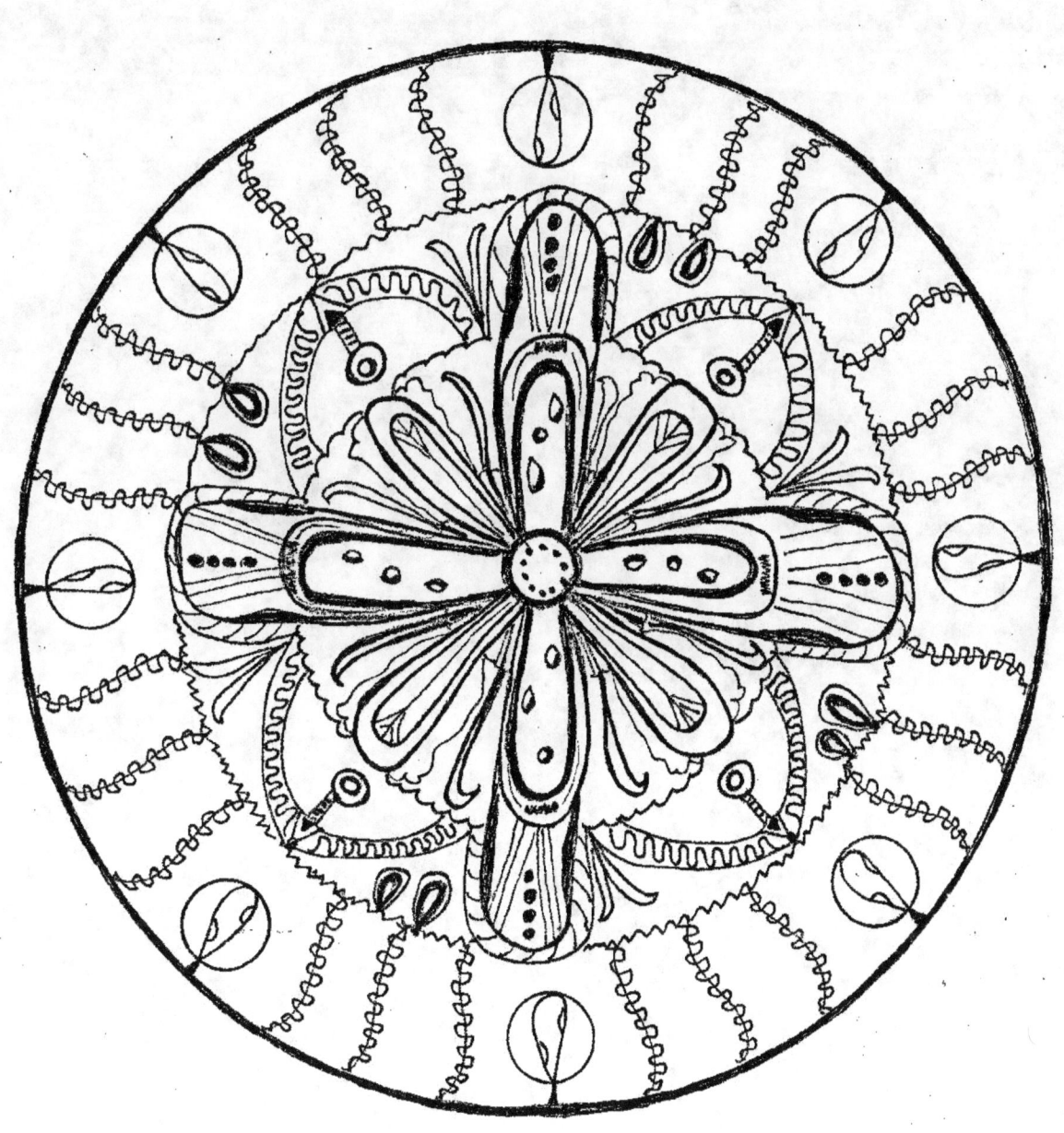

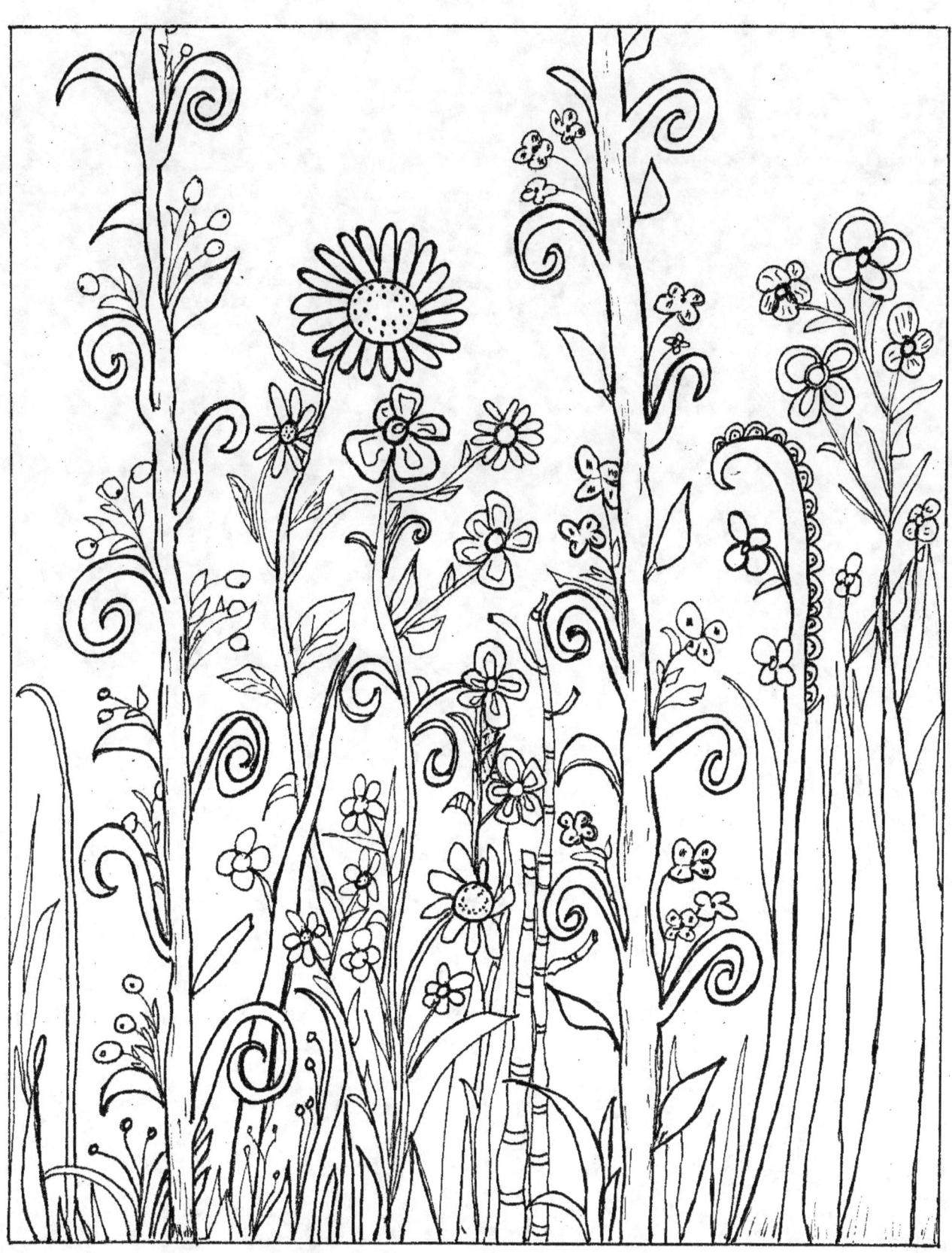

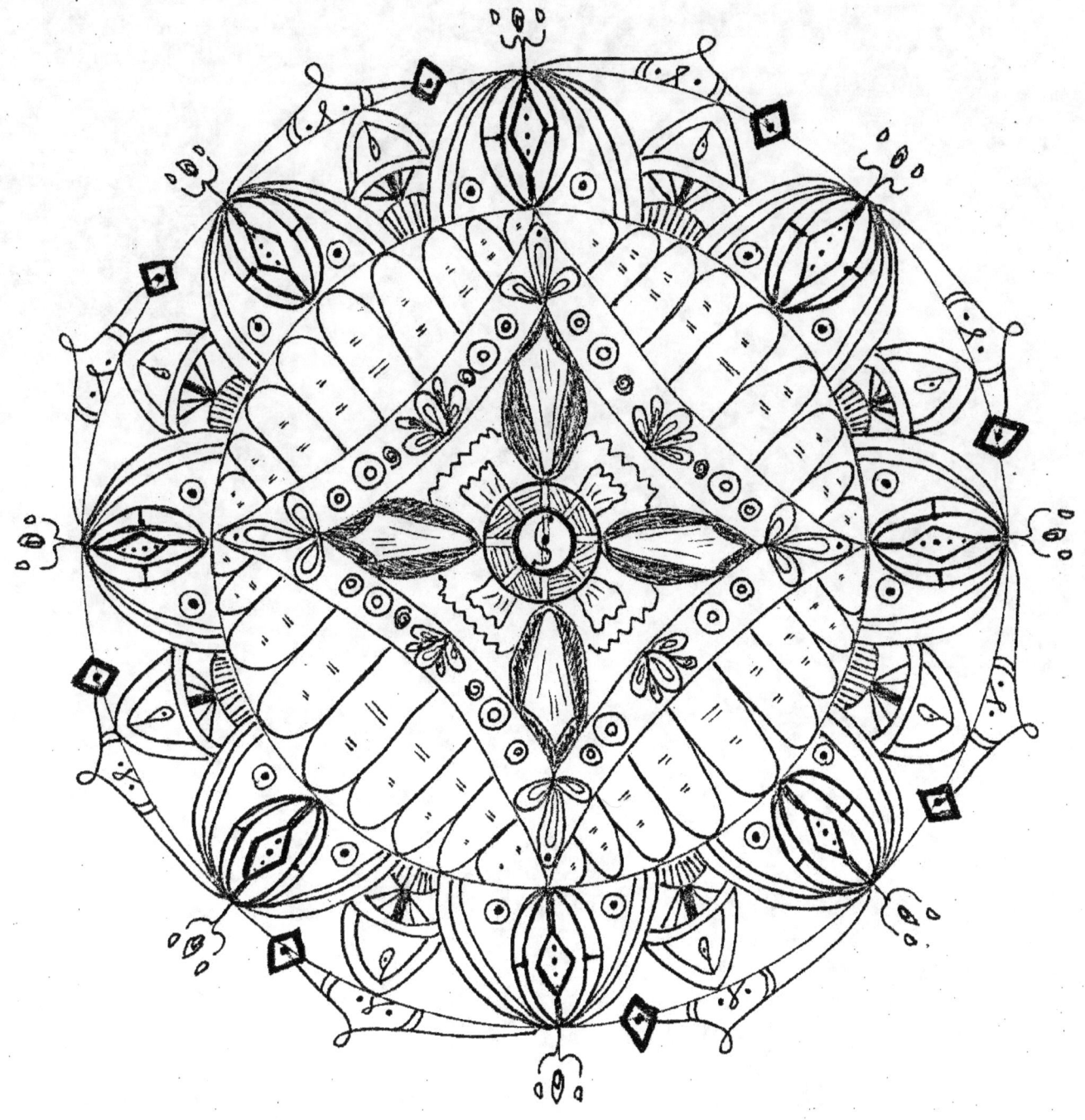

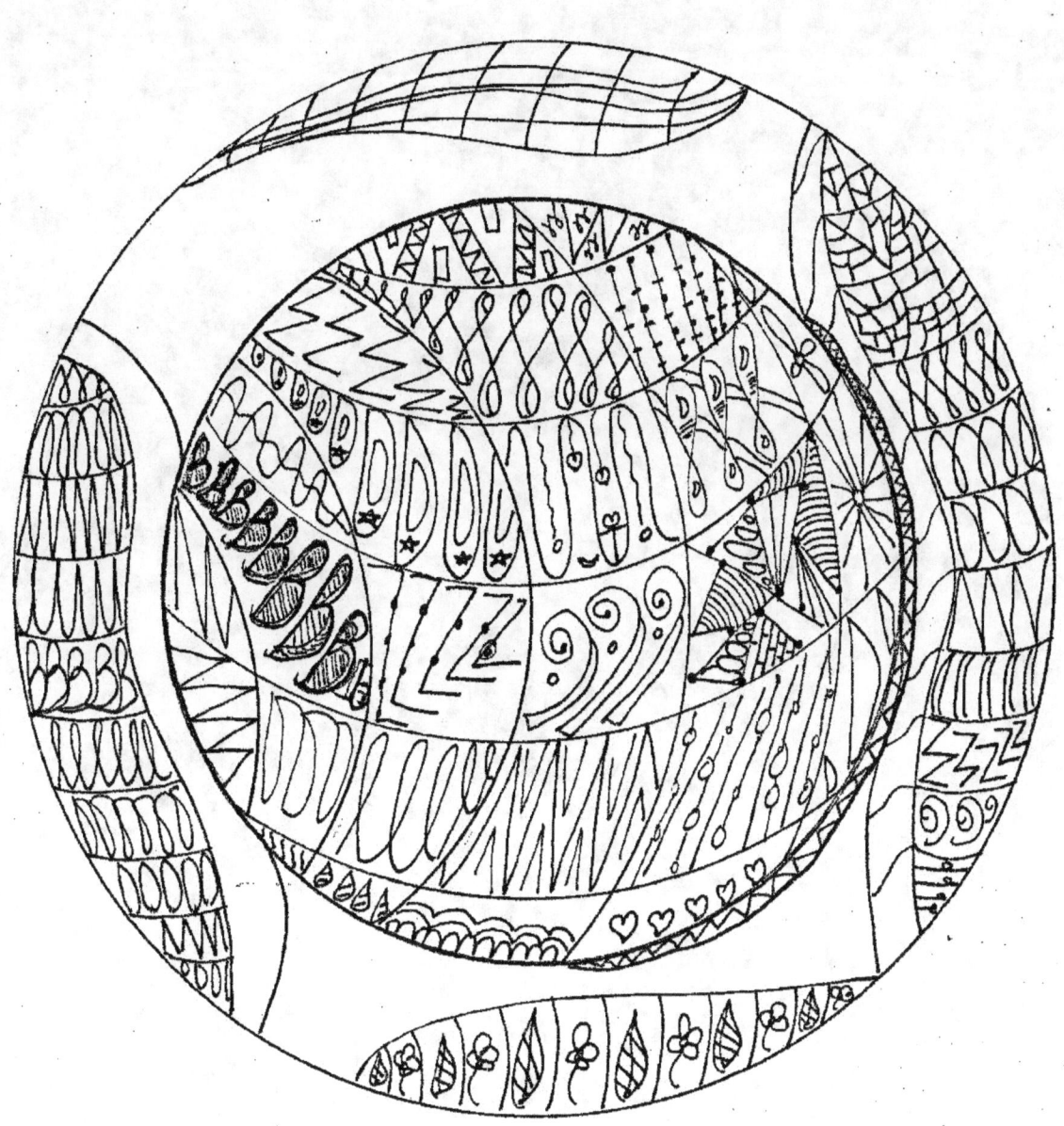

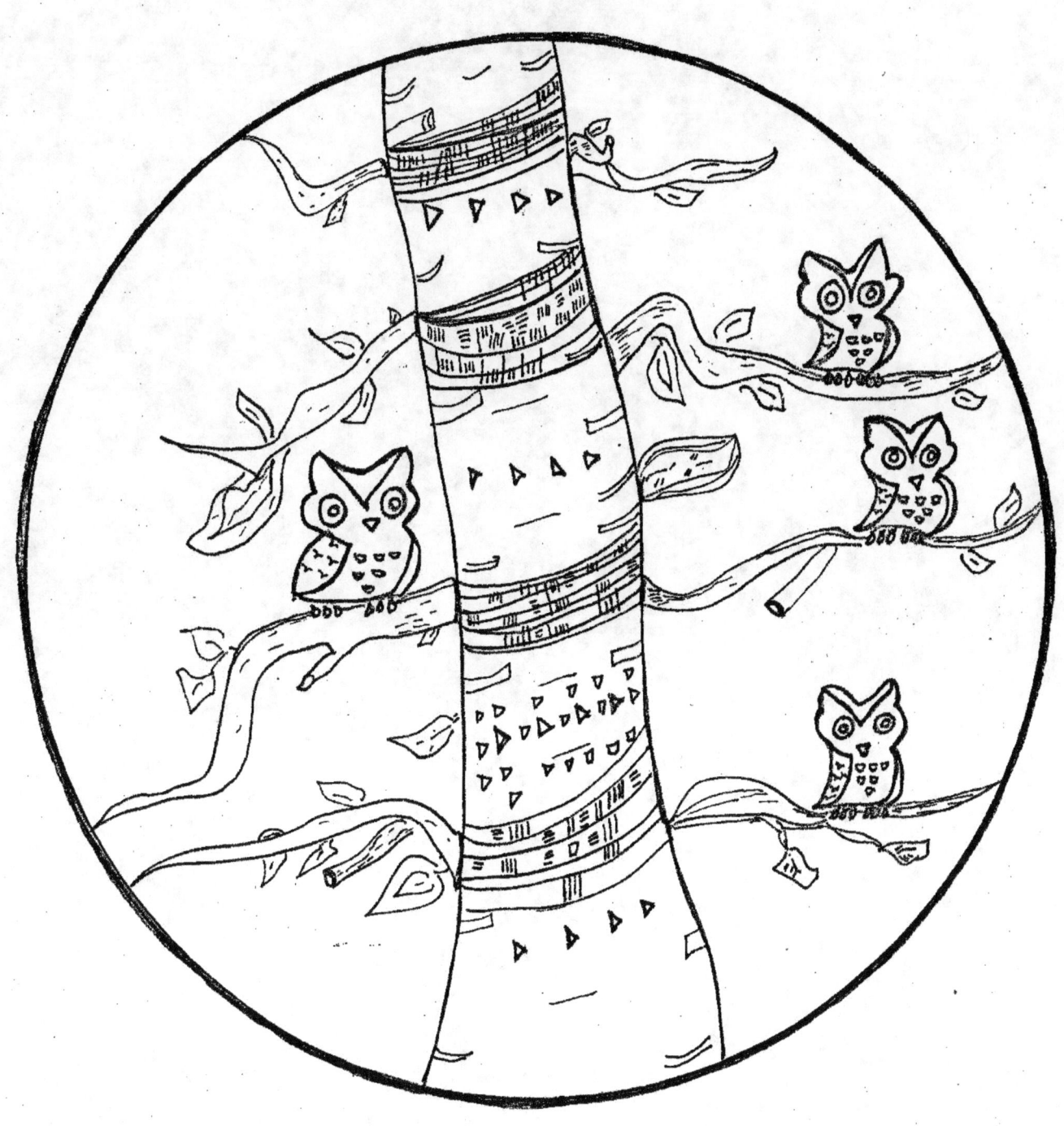

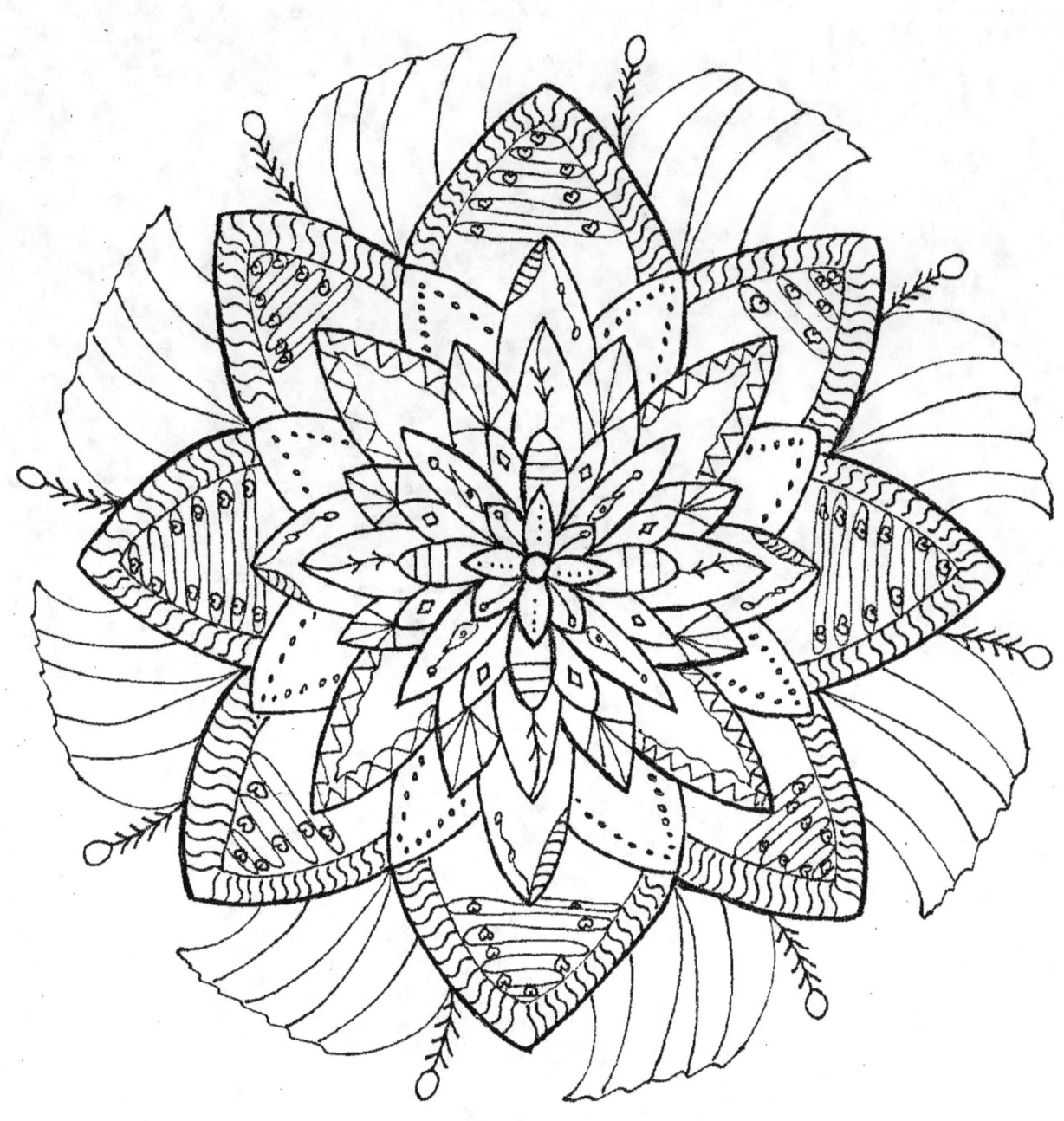

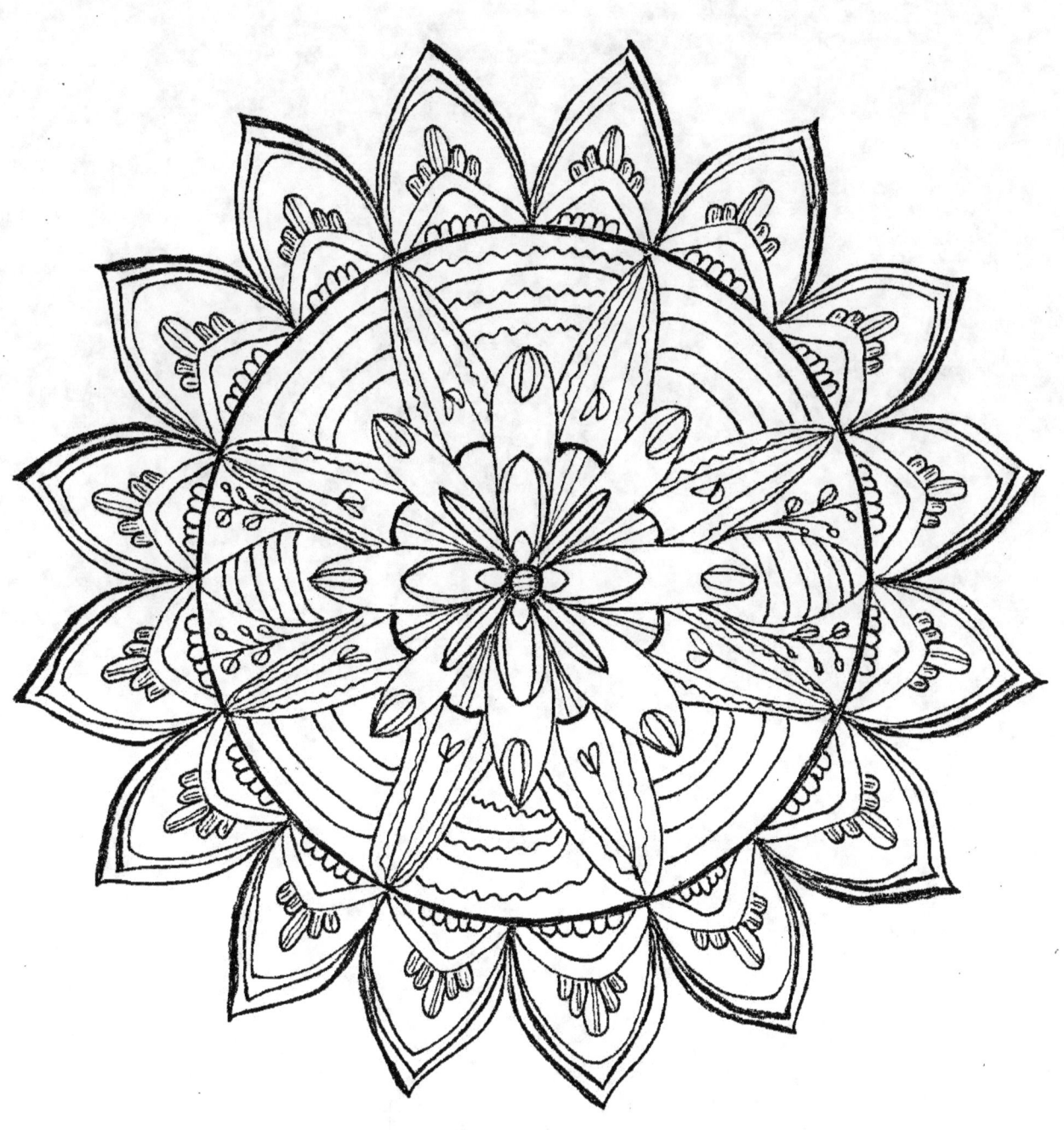

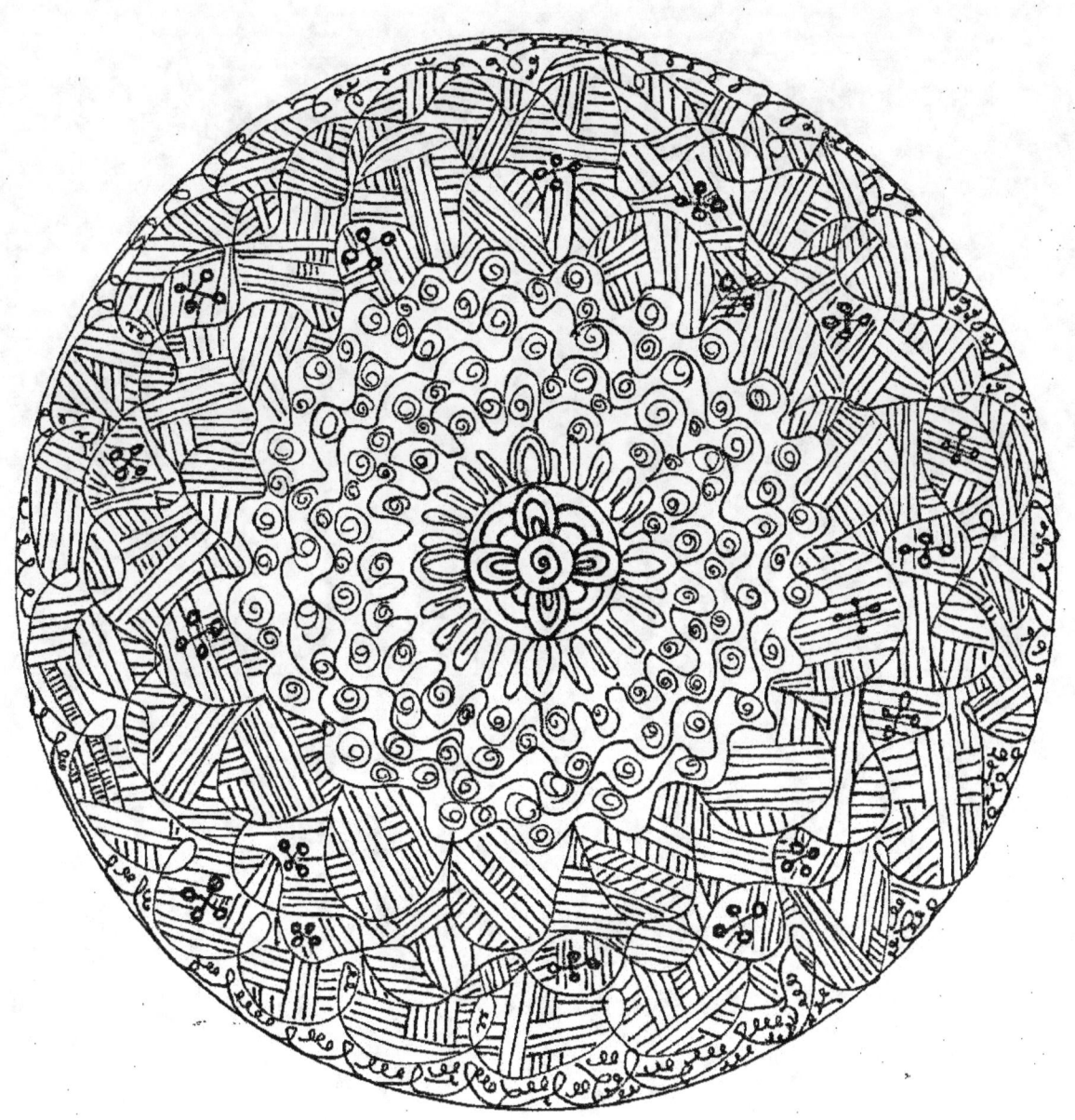

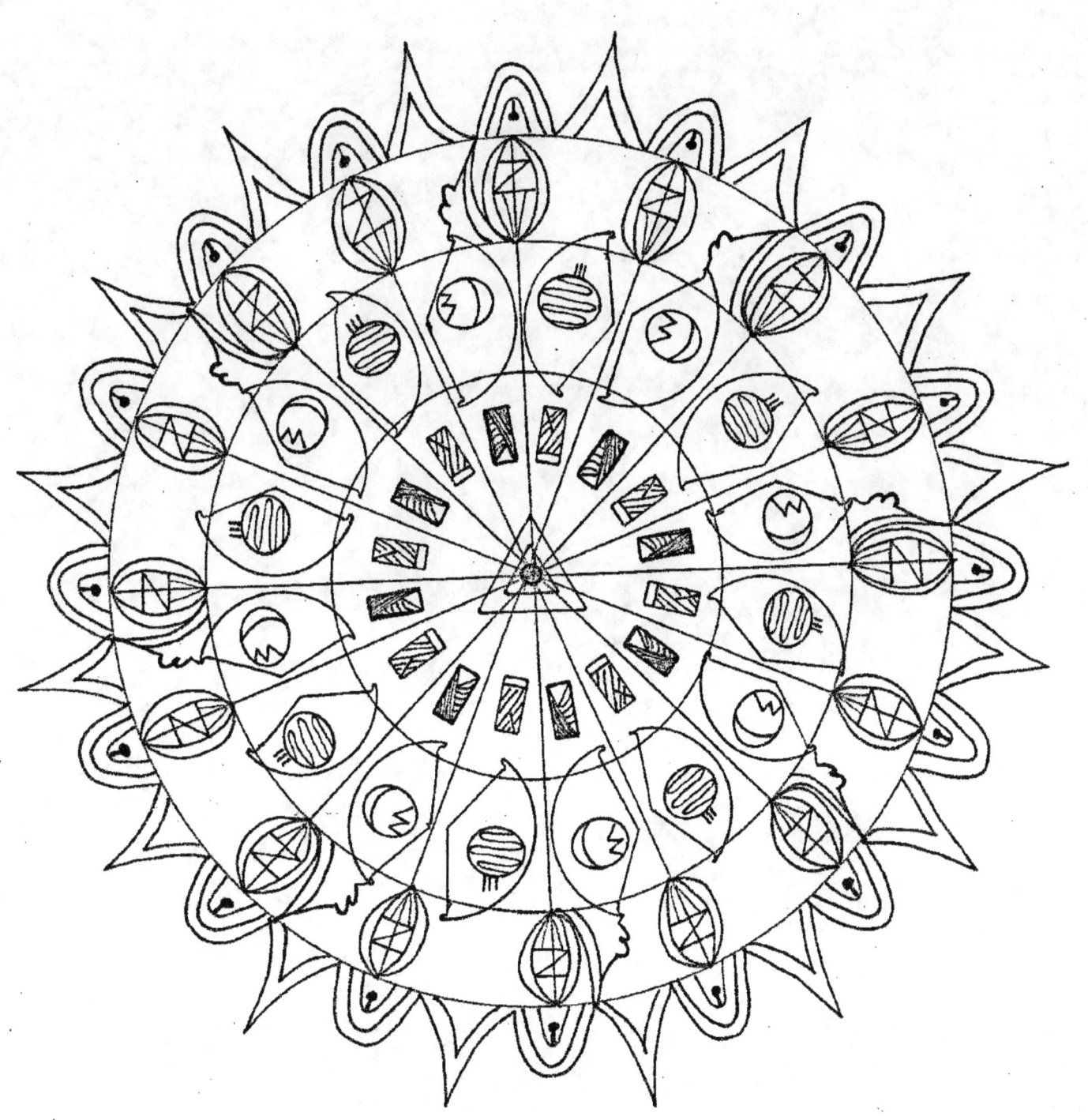

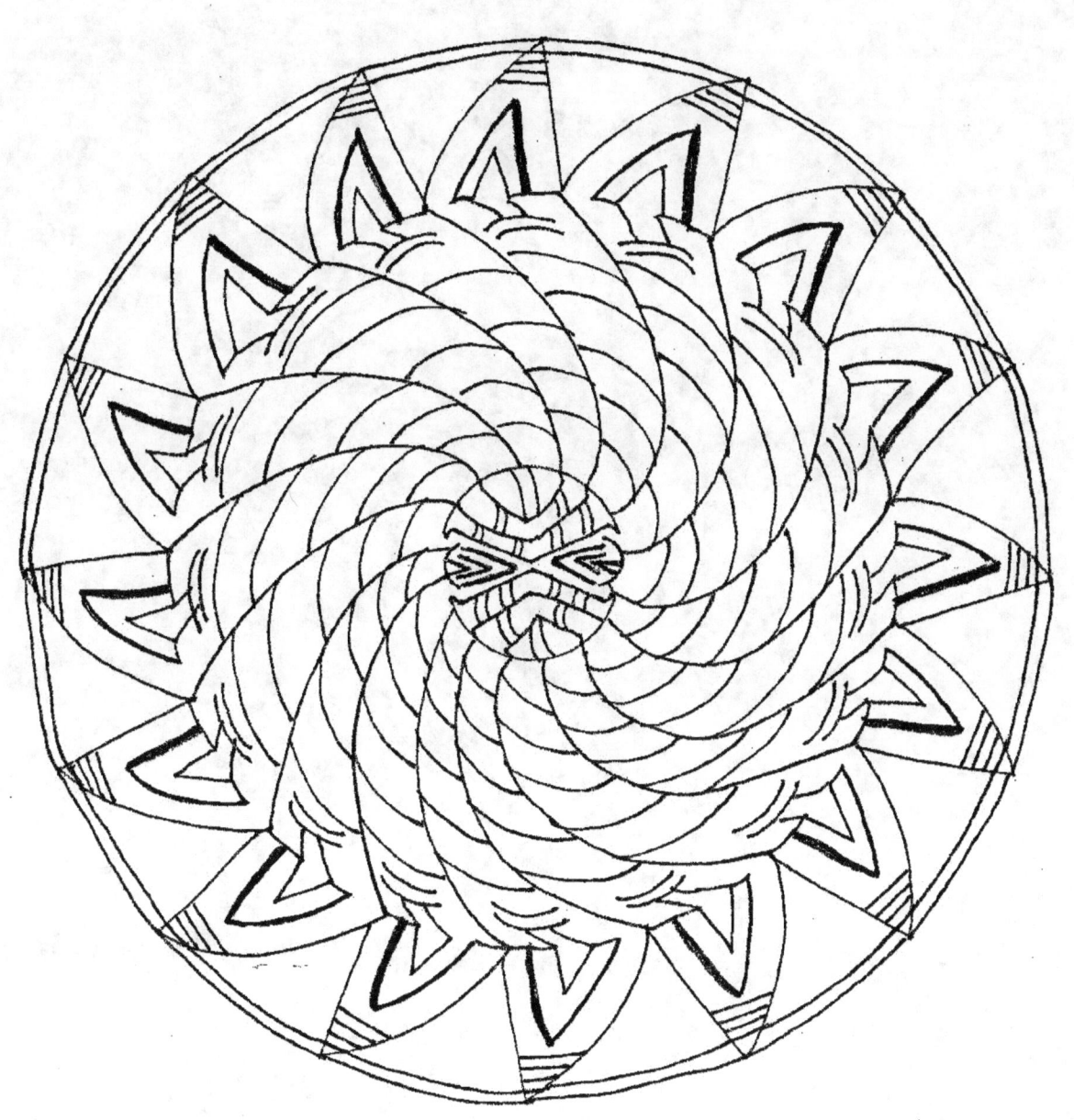

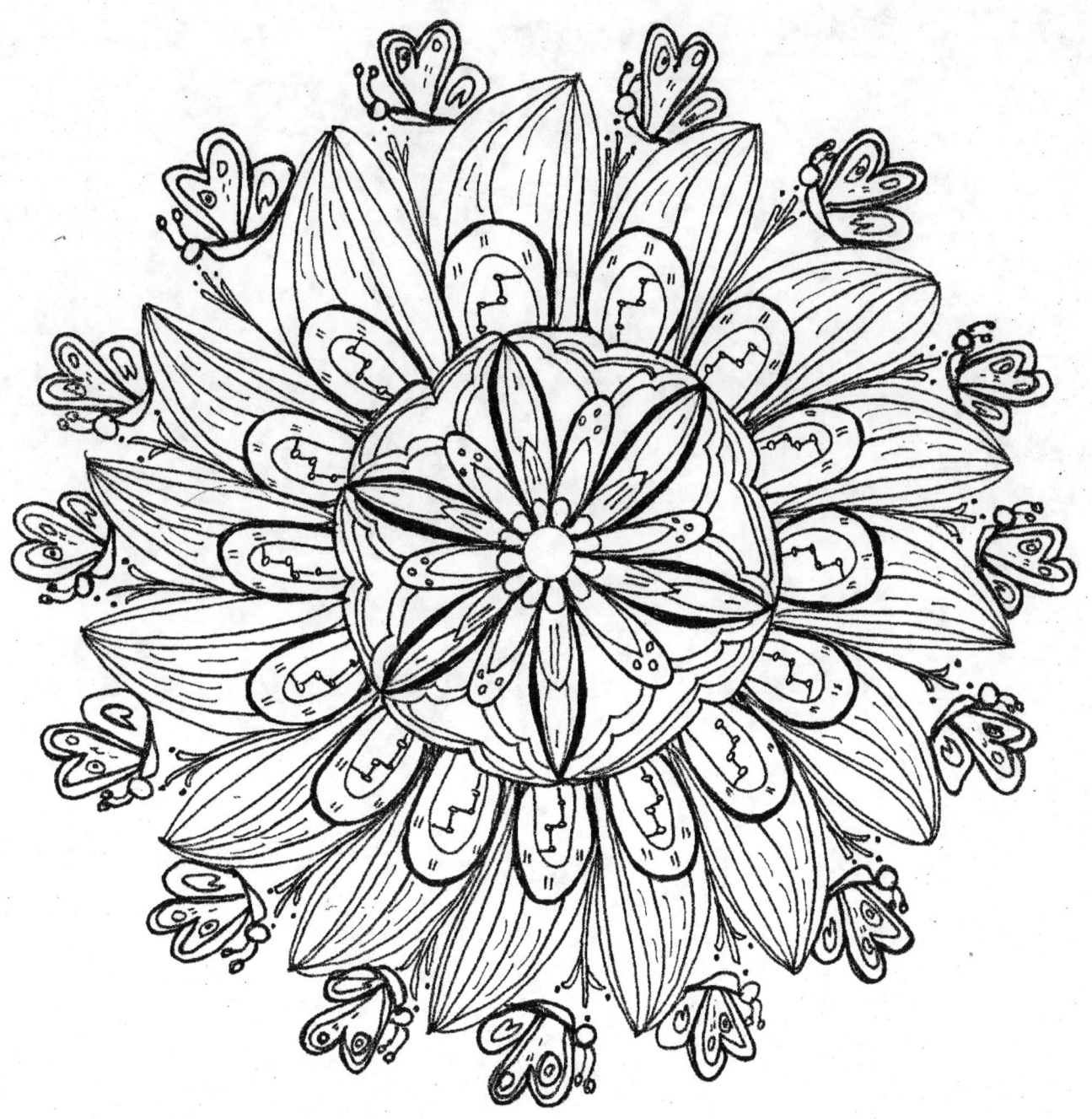

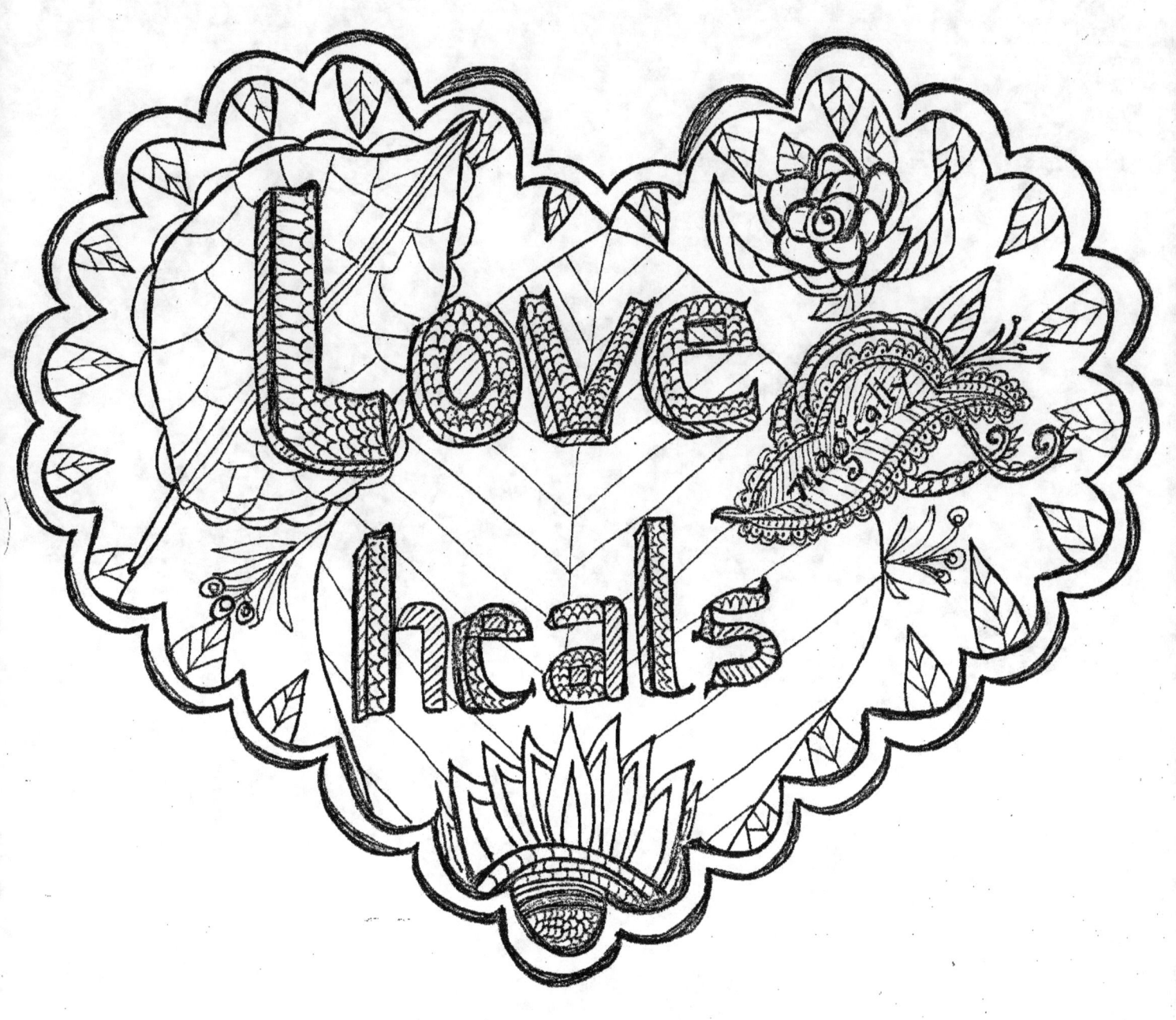

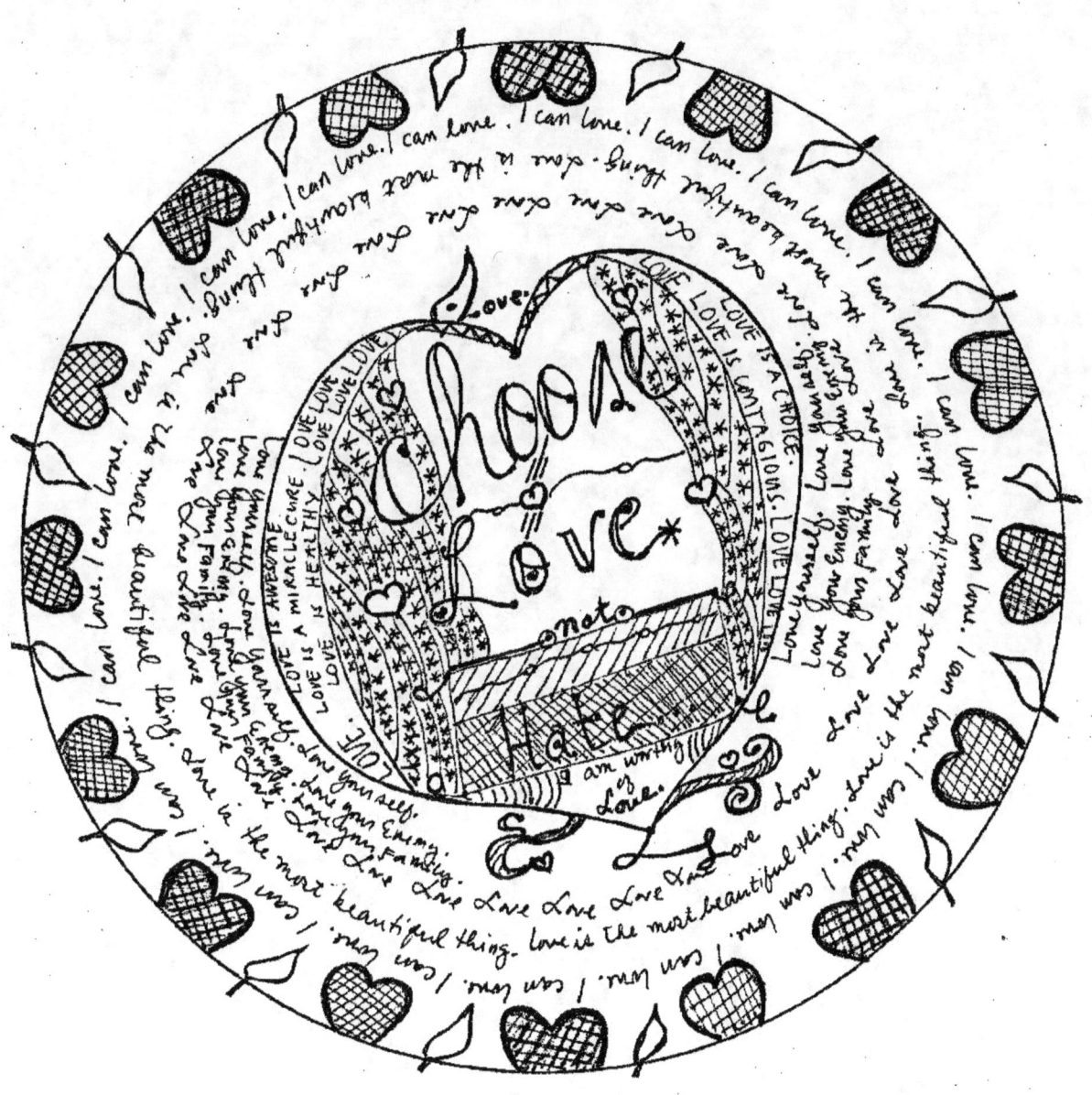